This book may be kept

FOURTEEN DAYS

A fine will be charged for each day the book is kept overtime.

OCT 14 1968	OCT 9 '72	
DEC 3 1968	Dec 15 '82	
JAN 22 1969	NOV 20 1984	
MAR 5 1969		
MAY 23 1969		
OCT 30 1969		
DEC 19 1969		
JAN 30 1970		
MAR 13 1970		
APR 24 1970		
OCT 23 1970		
DEC 18 1970		
FEB 17 1971		

GAYLORD 142

D1190958

A65500 378343

Poems for Pleasure

To see the world in a grain of sand,
 And a heaven in a wild flower;
Hold infinity in the palm of your hand,
 And eternity in an hour.

—WILLIAM BLAKE

Poems for Pleasure

Edited by

HERMAN M. WARD

36344

 HILL AND WANG · NEW YORK

FIRST EDITION MARCH 1963
SECOND PRINTING OCTOBER 1963
THIRD PRINTING APRIL 1964

To all young people entering the world of poetry

Manufactured in the United States of America by
The Colonial Press Inc., Clinton, Massachusetts

Acknowledgments

FOR permission to reprint these poems thanks are due the following poets, their copyright holders, and publishers:

Mrs. George Bambridge, Doubleday & Co., and The Macmillan Company of Canada Ltd.—for "Danny Deever" and "Gunga Din" from *Rudyard Kipling's Verse, Definitive Edition*; for "The Ballad of East and West" and "If" from *Rudyard Kipling's Verse*, copyright 1910 by Rudyard Kipling.

The Bobbs-Merrill Co.—for "When the Frost Is on the Punkin" from *Joyful Poems for Children* by James Whitcomb Riley, copyright © 1946, 1960 by The Bobbs-Merrill Co., Inc.

Jonathan Cape Ltd. and Mrs. H. M. Davies—for "Leisure" by W. H. Davies.

Chatto & Windus Ltd.—for "Dulce et Decorum Est" from *The Poems of Wilfred Owen*.

J. M. Dent & Sons Ltd.—for "The Force That Through the Green Fuse Drives" by Dylan Thomas.

Dodd, Mead & Co.—for "The Cremation of Sam McGee" from *The Spell of the Yukon* by Robert W. Service.

Doubleday & Co.—for "My Papa's Waltz" from *The Lost Son and Other Poems* by Theodore Roethke, copyright 1942 by Hearst Magazines, Inc.

Norma Millay Ellis—for "Renascence," "Spring," "Recuerdo," and "Afternoon on a Hill" from *Collected Poems* by Edna St. Vincent Millay, published by Harper & Brothers, copyright 1912, 1913, 1921, 1940, 1948 by Edna St. Vincent Millay, and 1954 by Norma Millay Ellis.

Faber & Faber Ltd.—for "Prayer Before Birth" from *Collected Poems* by Louis MacNeice; for "Musée des Beaux Arts" and "Stop All the Clocks" from *Collected Shorter Poems* by W. H. Auden.

Harcourt, Brace & World—for "in Just—" from *Poems 1923–1954* by E. E. Cummings, copyright 1923, 1951 by E. E. Cummings; for "Mia Carlotta" from *Selected Poems of T. A. Daly*, copyright 1936 by Harcourt, Brace & World, Inc.; for "Jazz Fantasia" from *Smoke and Steel* by Carl Sandburg, copyright 1920 by Harcourt, Brace & World, Inc.

The Belknap Press of Harvard University Press and the Trustees of Amherst College—for "A Day" and "The Snow"

Preface

STUDENTS should not be surprised if they find a good many of their favorite poems in this book. Several high school students collaborated with the editor last year, both in and out of class, and voted on the selections. They eliminated those that they did not like and chose most of the poems that are included. They were asked to select only those which "came right off the page" to them without benefit of teachers or critics. They were asked to stay away from poems that needed further study, or poems that they thought they *should* like. They were cautioned against "brand names" like Shakespeare, Keats, or Frost. Over and over again they were reminded that this was to be a book for enjoyment.

One evening at the editor's home eighteen tenth-graders sat around the living room and read poetry from seven thirty until ten thirty with a few breaks for cokes and cookies, and voted on about two thirds of the poems. Some of their comments were revealing. One girl said of "Little Boy Blue," "I know I'm not supposed to like it, but I do." Another asked, after reading "Aprilmonth," "Who is this fellow Bitterman? Do you have any more by him?" Another at the close of the evening remarked, "When can we do this again?" These were academic students who were planning to go on to college.

The poems were also submitted to two eleventh grade commercial classes and to one eleventh grade class of below average general students. It is surprising that their preferences were almost exactly the same as those of the academic students.

The editor then checked the choices with approximately forty high school teachers of his acquaintance and with fifty-five college students who were studying to be English teachers. He sought further confirmation of his choices in lists of the most popular poems for boys and girls, in the contents of other anthologies, and in casual conversations about poetry with teenagers whom he has the good fortune to know.

Some of the poems in this book are admittedly not great art. The editor has included them because he believes that the development of literary taste cannot be hurried; it must come slowly and honestly. There are no short cuts to it, though teachers from time immemorial have been annoyed with the poor taste of their students and have felt impelled to speed up the maturing process. "Poor" has often meant merely different, though sometimes it has stood for dishonest writing, illogical art, trite expression, stereotype imagery, or sing-song rhythm. However, the editor believes that until a reader sincerely prefers Keats's "Ode to Autumn" to James Whitcomb Riley's "When the Frost Is on the Punkin," there is nothing to be gained by deriding his choice; in fact, something may be lost. The editor remembers when he honestly preferred the latter poem. Indeed, he liked it so much he memorized it on his own. Today he cannot stand Riley and he prefers Keats. The change came about more slowly than most people would imagine. Derision might have turned him completely away from poetry. We should realize that there are some poems that seem to "live" just for young people and then are heard no more.

A glance at the Table of Contents will show that the young often prefer great poetry if they have had enough experience to understand it. However, there are practically no young people who would get genuine pleasure out of the later poems of Yeats. Even the poems whose preferences they share with adults are really liked for different reasons and from different vantage points.

The editor hopes that this book will, first of all, find its way into the libraries of teenagers and into their pockets as they go on trips or away to camp. He would be very happy to have them spend the kind of evening that those tenth-graders spent at his house and discover that an evening of poetry can be fun. He would like teachers and librarians to encourage students to own this book. He would like high schools to use it on any level as a supplementary book and with the idea that it is not only fun to read poetry but fun to read the same poems year after year and see how some of them grow in meaning and how others diminish in importance.

The arrangement of the poems in this book is quite unconventional. The editor has avoided listing them chronologically or alphabetically by author or by categories such as "adventure" or "love" poems or by types such as "dramatic" or "lyric" poetry. Rather, he has placed them in a carefully disorganized fashion so that the reader can open this book anywhere and read a half dozen or so selections on various subjects. In each "little package" there is usually a humorous or light piece of verse. In other words, the editor envisions a boy or girl reading and rereading this book a little bit at a time.

There is a second section in this book called "Poems for a Second Look." These poems have pleased a minority of teenagers. They are admittedly difficult reading. They demand more than one reading. But they are satisfying when one gets to know them. They should be tried occasionally.

Above all, the editor hopes that this book will be *enjoyed* by young people!

The editor wishes to thank Mr. William Cook and Miss Mary Perpetua of the English Department of Princeton High School, Princeton, New Jersey, and the many students of that school who helped with the preparation of this book. He also thanks the college students of Trenton State College and the many English teachers of the State of New Jersey for their suggestions. He is grateful to the students he taught in his early years of teaching at Bloomfield High School, Hasbrouck Heights High School, and Millburn High School, who showed him that teenagers could be genuinely interested in poetry if they were given, or were allowed to select, poems that were meaningful to them. And last but not least, he sends a deep expression of gratitude to Mrs. Edith Belitza, who tirelessly helped with the typing of the manuscript.

HERMAN M. WARD

Contents

POEMS FOR A SECOND LOOK

xvi

Poems for Pleasure

Admonition

Close not your door on life.
Life is the bright outside,
The sun and happiness,
The giddy laughter of a frivolous brook,
The din of waterfalls,
The happy imperfection of a thornèd rose,
An echo from a mountainside.

Within dark portals
Dingy walls of dread
Confine but selfishness.

Lock not your door on life:
Keys are too easily lost.

—HERBERT BITTERMAN

When I Was One-and-Twenty

When I was one-and-twenty
  I heard a wise man say,
"Give crowns and pounds and guineas
  But not your heart away;
Give pearls away and rubies
  But keep your fancy free."
But I was one-and-twenty,
  No use to talk to me.

When I was one-and-twenty
  I heard him say again,
"The heart out of the bosom
  Was never given in vain;
'Tis paid with sighs a-plenty
  And sold for endless rue."
And I am two-and-twenty,
  And oh, 'tis true, 'tis true.

—A. E. HOUSMAN

1

Jazz Fantasia

Drum on your drums, batter on your banjos, sob on the
long cool winding saxophones. Go to it, O jazzmen.

Sling your knuckles on the bottoms of the happy tin pans,
let your trombones ooze, and go husha-husha-hush
with the slippery sandpaper.

Moan like an autumn wind high in the lonesome treetops,
moan soft like you wanted somebody terrible, cry
like a racing car slipping away from a motorcycle-
cop, bang-bang! you jazzmen, bang altogether
drums, traps, banjos, horns, tin cans—make two
people fight on the top of a stairway and scratch
each other's eyes in a clinch tumbling down the
stairs.

Can the rough stuff . . . Now a Mississippi steamboat
pushes up the night river with a hoo-hoo-hoo-oo
. . . and the green lanterns calling to the high soft
stars . . . a red moon rides on the humps of the
low river hills. . . . Go to it, O jazzmen.

—CARL SANDBURG

Résumé

Razors pain you;
Rivers are damp;
Acids stain you;
And drugs cause cramp.
Guns aren't lawful;
Nooses give;
Gas smells awful;
You might as well live.

—DOROTHY PARKER

The Creation

(A NEGRO SERMON)

And God stepped out on space,
And He looked around and said,
"I'm lonely—
I'll make a world."
And far as the eye of God could see
Darkness covered everything,
Blacker than a hundred midnights
Down in a cypress swamp.

Then God smiled,
And the light broke,
And the darkness rolled up on one side,
And the light stood shining on the other,
And God said, *"That's good!"*

Then God reached out and took the light in His hands,
And God rolled the light around in His hands,
Until He made the sun;
And He set that sun a-blazing in the heavens.
And the light that was left from making the sun
God gathered up in a shining ball
And flung against the darkness,
Spangling the night with the moon and stars.
Then down between
The darkness and the light
He hurled the world;
And God said, *"That's good!"*

Then God himself stepped down—
And the sun was on His right hand,
And the moon was on His left;
The stars were clustered about His head,
And the earth was under His feet.
And God walked, and where He trod
His footsteps hollowed the valleys out
And bulged the mountains up.

Then He stopped and looked and saw
That the earth was hot and barren.

So God stepped over to the edge of the world
And He spat out the seven seas;
He batted His eyes, and the lightnings flashed;
He clapped His hands, and the thunders rolled;
And the waters above the earth came down,
The cooling waters came down.

Then the green grass sprouted,
And the little red flowers blossomed,
The pine tree pointed his finger to the sky,
And the oak spread out his arms;
The lakes cuddled down in the hollows of the ground,
And the rivers ran down to the sea;
And God smiled again,
And the rainbow appeared,
And curled itself around His shoulder.

Then God raised His arm and He waved His hand
Over the sea and over the land,
And He said, *"Bring forth! Bring forth!"*
And quicker than God could drop His hand,
Fishes and fowls
And beasts and birds
Swam the rivers and the seas,
Roamed the forests and the woods,
And split the air with their wings,
And God said, *"That's good!"*

Then God walked around
And God looked around
On all that He had made.
He looked at His sun,
And He looked at His moon,
And He looked at His little stars;
He looked on His world
With all its living things,
And God said, *"I'm lonely still."*

Then God sat down
On the side of a hill where He could think;
By a deep, wide river He sat down;
With His head in His hands,
God thought and thought,
Till He thought, *"I'll make me a man!"*

4

Up from the bed of the river
God scooped the clay;
And by the bank of the river
He kneeled Him down;
And there the great God Almighty,
Who lit the sun and fixed it in the sky,
Who flung the stars to the most far corner of the night,
Who rounded the earth in the middle of His hand—
This Great God,
Like a mammy bending over her baby,
Kneeled down in the dust
Toiling over a lump of clay
Till He shaped it in His own image;
Then into it He blew the breath of life,
And man became a living soul.
Amen. Amen.

—James Weldon Johnson

Invictus

Out of the night that covers me,
    Black as the Pit from pole to pole,
I thank whatever gods may be
    For my unconquerable soul.

In the fell clutch of circumstance
    I have not winced nor cried aloud.
Under the bludgeonings of chance
    My head is bloody, but unbowed.

Beyond this place of wrath and tears
    Looms but the horror of the shade,
And yet the menace of the years
    Finds, and shall find, me unafraid.

It matters not how strait the gate,
    How charged with punishments the scroll,
I am the master of my fate:
    I am the captain of my soul.

—William Ernest Henley

Pippa's Song

The year's at the spring
And day's at the morn;
Morning's at seven;
The hill-side's dew-pearled;
The lark's on the wing;
The snail's on the thorn:
God's in his heaven—
All's right with the world!

—ROBERT BROWNING

A Dirge

Rough wind, that moanest loud
   Grief too sad for song;
Wild wind, when sullen cloud
   Knells all the night long;
Sad storm, whose tears are vain,
Bare woods, whose branches strain,
Deep caves and dreary main,
   Wail, for the world's wrong!

—PERCY BYSSHE SHELLEY

The Shell

And then I pressed the shell
Close to my ear
And listened well,
And straightway like a bell
Came low and clear
The slow, sad murmur of the distant seas,
Whipped by an icy breeze
Upon a shore
Wind-swept and desolate.

6

It was a sunless strand that never bore
The footprint of a man,
Nor felt the weight
Since time began
Of any human quality or stir
Save what the dreary winds and waves incur.
And in the hush of waters was the sound
Of pebbles rolling round,
Forever rolling with a hollow sound.
And bubbling seaweeds as the waters go
Swish to and fro
Their long, cold tentacles of slimy gray.
There was no day,
Nor ever came a night
Setting the stars alight
To wonder at the moon:
Was twilight only and the frightened croon,
Smitten to whimpers, of the dreary wind
And waves that journeyed blind—
And then I loosed my ear . . . O, it was sweet
To hear a cart go jolting down the street.

—JAMES STEPHENS

Abou Ben Adhem

Abou Ben Adhem (may his tribe increase!)
Awoke one night from a deep dream of peace,
And saw within the moonlight in his room,
Making it rich and like a lily in bloom,
An angel writing in a book of gold:
Exceeding peace had made Ben Adhem bold,
And to the presence in the room he said,
"What writest thou?" The vision raised its head,
And, with a look made of all sweet accord,
Answered, "The names of those who love the Lord."
"And is mine one?" said Abou. "Nay, not so,"
Replied the angel. Abou spoke more low,
But cheerily still; and said, "I pray thee, then,
Write me as one that loves his fellow men."

7

The angel wrote, and vanished. The next night
It came again, with a great wakening light,
And showed the names whom love of God had blessed,—
And, lo! Ben Adhem's name led all the rest!

—LEIGH HUNT

Casey at the Bat

It looked extremely rocky for the Mudville nine that day,
The score stood four to six with but an inning left to play.
And so, when Cooney died at first, and Burrows did the
    same,
A pallor wreathed the features of the patrons of the game.
A straggling few got up to go, leaving there the rest,
With that hope which springs eternal within the human
    breast.
For they thought if only Casey could get a whack at that,
They'd put up even money with Casey at the bat.
But Flynn preceded Casey, and likewise so did Blake,
And the former was a pudding and the latter was a fake;
So on that stricken multitude a deathlike silence sat,
For there seemed but little chance of Casey's getting to
    the bat.
But Flynn let drive a single to the wonderment of all,
And the much despisèd Blakey tore the cover off the ball,
And when the dust had lifted and they saw what had
    occurred,
There was Blakey safe on second, and Flynn a-hugging
    third.
Then from the gladdened multitude went up a joyous yell,
It bounded from the mountain top and rattled in the dell,
It struck upon the hillside, and rebounded on the flat,
For Casey, mighty Casey, was advancing to the bat.
There was ease in Casey's manner as he stepped into his
    place,
There was pride in Casey's bearing and a smile on Casey's
    face,
And when responding to the cheers he lightly doffed his
    hat,

No stranger in the crowd could doubt, 'twas Casey at the
bat.

Ten thousand eyes were on him as he rubbed his hands
with dirt,

Five thousand tongues applauded as he wiped them on
his shirt;

And while the writhing pitcher ground the ball into his
hip—

Defiance gleamed from Casey's eye—a sneer curled Casey's
lip.

And now the leather-covered sphere came hurtling through
the air,

And Casey stood a-watching it in haughty grandeur there;

Close by the sturdy batsman the ball unheeded sped—

"That hain't my style," said Casey—"Strike one," the
Umpire said.

From the bleachers black with people there rose a sullen
roar,

Like the beating of the storm waves on a stern and distant
shore,

"Kill him! kill the Umpire!" shouted someone from the
stand—

And it's likely they'd have done it had not Casey raised
his hand.

With a smile of Christian charity great Casey's visage
shone,

He stilled the rising tumult and he bade the game go on;

He signaled to the pitcher and again the spheroid flew,

But Casey still ignored it and the Umpire said, "Strike
two."

"Fraud!" yelled the maddened thousands, and the echo
answered "Fraud."

But one scornful look from Casey and the audience was
awed;

They saw his face grow stern and cold; they saw his
muscles strain,

And they knew that Casey would not let that ball go by
again.

The sneer is gone from Casey's lip; his teeth are clenched
with hate,

He pounds with cruel violence his bat upon the plate;

And now the pitcher holds the ball, and now he lets it go,

And now the air is shattered by the force of Casey's blow.

Oh! somewhere in this favored land the sun is shining
   bright,
The band is playing somewhere, and somewhere hearts are
   light,
And somewhere men are laughing, and somewhere chil-
   dren shout;
But there is no joy in Mudville—mighty Casey has Struck
   Out.

—ERNEST LAWRENCE THAYER

The Listeners

"Is there anybody there?" said the Traveler,
   Knocking on the moonlit door;
And his horse in the silence champed the grasses
   Of the forest's ferny floor:
And a bird flew up out of the turret,
   Above the Traveler's head:
And he smote upon the door again a second time;
   "Is there anybody there?" he said.
But no one descended to the Traveler;
   No head from the leaf-fringed sill
Leaned over and looked into his gray eyes,
   Where he stood perplexed and still.
But only a host of phantom listeners
   That dwelt in the lone house then
Stood listening in the quiet of the moonlight
   To that voice from the world of men:
Stood thronging the faint moon beams on the dark stair,
   That goes down to the empty hall,
Hearkening in an air stirred and shaken
   By the lonely Traveler's call.
And he felt in his heart their strangeness,
   Their stillness answering his cry,
While his horse moved, cropping the dark turf,
   'Neath the starred and leafy sky;
For he suddenly smote on the door, even
   Louder, and lifted his head:—
"Tell them I came, and no one answered,
   That I kept my word," he said.

10

Never the least stir made the listeners,
 Though every word he spake
Fell echoing through the shadowiness of the still house
 From the one man left awake:
Ay, they heard his foot upon the stirrup,
 And the sound of iron on stone
And how the silence surged softly backward
 When the plunging hoofs were gone.

     —WALTER DE LA MARE

The Bells

I

 Hear the sledges with the bells—
  Silver bells!
What a world of merriment their melody foretells!
 How they tinkle, tinkle, tinkle,
  In the icy air of night!
 While the stars that oversprinkle
 All the heavens, seem to twinkle
  With a crystalline delight;
 Keeping time, time, time,
 In a sort of Runic rhyme,
To the tintinnabulation that so musically wells
 From the bells, bells, bells, bells,
  Bells, bells, bells—
From the jingling and the tinkling of the bells.

II

 Hear the mellow wedding bells—
  Golden bells!
What a world of happiness their harmony foretells!
  Through the balmy air of night
 How they ring out their delight!—
  From the molten-golden notes,
  And all in tune,
 What a liquid ditty floats
To the turtledove that listens, while she gloats
  On the moon!
 Oh, from out the sounding cells,

What a gush of euphony voluminously wells!
How it swells!
How it dwells
On the Future!—how it tells
Of the rapture that impels
To the swinging and the ringing
Of the bells, bells, bells—
Of the bells, bells, bells, bells,
Bells, bells, bells—
To the rhyming and the chiming of the bells!

III

Hear the loud alarum bells—
Brazen bells!
What a tale of terror, now their turbulency tells!
In the startled ear of night
How they scream out their affright!
Too much horrified to speak,
They can only shriek, shriek,
Out of tune,
In a clamorous appealing to the mercy of the fire,
In a mad expostulation with the deaf and frantic fire,
Leaping higher, higher, higher,
With a desperate desire,
And a resolute endeavor
Now—now to sit, or never,
By the side of the pale-faced moon.
Oh, the bells, bells, bells!
What a tale their terror tells
Of Despair!
How they clang, and clash, and roar!
What a horror they outpour
On the bosom of the palpitating air!
Yet the ear, it fully knows,
By the twanging,
And the clanging,
How the danger ebbs and flows;
Yet the ear distinctly tells,
In the jangling,
And the wrangling,
How the danger sinks and swells,
By the sinking or the swelling in the anger of the bells—
Of the bells—

Of the bells, bells, bells, bells,
        Bells, bells, bells—
In the clamor and the clangor of the bells!

IV

Hear the tolling of the bells—
        Iron bells!
What a world of solemn thought their monody compels!
        In the silence of the night,
        How we shiver with affright
At the melancholy menace of their tone!
        For every sound that floats
        From the rust within their throats
                Is a groan.
And the people—ah, the people—
They that dwell up in the steeple,
        All alone,
And who, tolling, tolling, tolling,
        In that muffled monotone,
Feel a glory in so rolling
        On the human heart a stone—
They are neither man nor woman—
They are neither brute nor human—
        They are Ghouls:—
And their king it is who tolls:—
And he rolls, rolls, rolls,
        Rolls
        A paean from the bells!
And his merry bosom swells
        With the paean of the bells!
And he dances, and he yells;
Keeping time, time, time,
In a sort of Runic rhyme,

To the paean of the bells:—
        Of the bells:
Keeping time, time, time,
In a sort of Runic rhyme,
        To the throbbing of the bells—
Of the bells, bells, bells—
        To the sobbing of the bells:—
Keeping time, time, time,
        As he knells, knells, knells,

13

In a happy Runic rhyme,
  To the rolling of the bells—
Of the bells, bells, bells:—
  To the tolling of the bells—
Of the bells, bells, bells, bells,
    Bells, bells, bells—
To the moaning and the groaning of the bells.
                    —EDGAR ALLAN POE

Pied Beauty

Glory be to God for dappled things—
  For skies of couple-color as a brinded cow;
    For rose-moles all in stipple upon trout that swim;
Fresh-firecoal chestnut-falls; finches' wings;
  Landscape plotted and pieced—fold, fallow, and plow;
    And áll trádes, their gear and tackle and trim.

All things counter, original, spare, strange;
  Whatever is fickle, freckled (who knows how?)
    With swift, slow; sweet, sour; adazzle, dim;
He fathers-forth whose beauty is past change:
          Praise him.
                —GERARD MANLEY HOPKINS

Last Dance of the Leaves

Dead leaves skidding the chill macadam,
Whipped by the wind into sudden circles,
Scudding dryly, crisply, hoarsely,
Rasp of voices in croaked pizzicato—

  Breath of the moon in the starlight frozen,
  Chilling the leaves to sterile silence;
  Once they were green, and red, and orange,
  Now frozen yellow-brown-yellow-brown-yellow—

14

Once the living
Now the dying
All join hands
Join hands in a circle
Scudding and skidding the trackless pavement,
Yellow-brown-yellow-brown-yellow-brown-yellow.

—HERBERT BITTERMAN

To an Athlete Dying Young

The time you won your town the race
We chaired you through the market place;
Man and boy stood cheering by,
And home we brought you shoulder-high.

Today, the road all runners come,
Shoulder-high we bring you home,
And set you at your threshold down,
Townsman of a stiller town.

Smart lad, to slip betimes away
From fields where glory does not stay,
And early though the laurel grows
It withers quicker than the rose.

Eyes the shady night has shut
Cannot see the record cut,
And silence sounds no worse than cheers
After earth has stopped the ears:

Now you will not swell the rout
Of lads that wore their honors out,
Runners whom renown outran
And the name died before the man.

So set, before its echoes fade,
The fleet foot on the sill of shade,
And hold to the low lintel up
The still-defended challenge-cup.

And round that early-laureled head
Will flock to gaze the strengthless dead,
And find unwithered on its curls
The garland briefer than a girl's.

—A. E. Housman

Annabel Lee

It was many and many a year ago,
   In a kingdom by the sea,
That a maiden there lived, whom you may know
   By the name of Annabel Lee;
And this maiden she lived with no other thought
   Than to love, and be loved by me.

I was a child and she was a child,
   In this kingdom by the sea;
But we loved with a love that was more than love,
   I and my Annabel Lee,—
With a love that the wingèd seraphs of heaven
   Coveted her and me.

And this was the reason that long ago,
   In this kingdom by the sea,
A wind blew out of a cloud, chilling
   My beautiful Annabel Lee;
So that her highborn kinsmen came,
   And bore her away from me,
To shut her up in a sepulchre,
   In this kingdom by the sea.

The angels, not half so happy in heaven,
   Went envying her and me.
Yes! that was the reason (as all men know)
   In this kingdom by the sea,
That the wind came out of the cloud by night,
   Chilling and killing my Annabel Lee.

But our love it was stronger by far than the love
   Of those who were older than we,

Of many far wiser than we;
And neither the angels in heaven above,
  Nor the demons down under the sea,
Can ever dissever my soul from the soul
  Of the beautiful Annabel Lee.

For the moon never beams without bringing me dreams
  Of the beautiful Annabel Lee,
And the stars never rise but I feel the bright eyes
  Of the beautiful Annabel Lee.
And so, all the nighttide I lie down by the side
Of my darling, my darling, my life, and my bride,
  In her sepulchre there by the sea,
  In her tomb by the sounding sea.

—EDGAR ALLAN POE

How Do I Love Thee

How do I love thee? Let me count the ways.
I love thee to the depth and breadth and height
My soul can reach, when feeling out of sight
For the ends of Being and ideal Grace.
I love thee to the level of everyday's
Most quiet need, by sun and candlelight.
I love thee freely, as men strive for Right;
I love thee purely, as they turn from Praise.
I love thee with the passion put to use
In my old griefs, and with my childhood's faith.
I love thee with a love I seemed to lose
With my lost saints,—I love thee with the breath,
Smiles, tears, of all my life!—and, if God choose,
I shall but love thee better after death.

—ELIZABETH BARRETT BROWNING

The Rich Man

The rich man has his motorcar,
　His country and his town estate.
He smokes a fifty-cent cigar
　And jeers at Fate.

He frivols through the livelong day,
　He knows not Poverty, her pinch.
His lot seems light, his heart seems gay;
　He has a cinch.

Yet though my lamp burns low and dim,
　Though I must slave for livelihood—
Think you that I would change with him?
　You bet I would!

　　　　　　　　—Franklin P. Adams

The Daffodils

I wandered lonely as a cloud
That floats on high o'er vales and hills,
When all at once I saw a crowd,
A host, of golden daffodils;
Beside the lake, beneath the trees,
Fluttering and dancing in the breeze.

Continuous as the stars that shine
And twinkle on the milky way,
They stretched in never-ending line
Along the margin of a bay:
Ten thousand saw I at a glance,
Tossing their heads in sprightly dance.

The waves beside them danced; but they
Outdid the sparkling waves in glee:
A poet could not but be gay,
In such a jocund company:
I gazed—and gazed—but little thought
What wealth the show to me had brought:

For oft, when on my couch I lie
In vacant or in pensive mood,
They flash upon that inward eye
Which is the bliss of solitude;
And then my heart with pleasure fills,
And dances with the daffodils.

—WILLIAM WORDSWORTH

Four Little Foxes

Speak gently, Spring, and make no sudden sound;
For in my windy valley, yesterday I found
Newborn foxes squirming on the ground . . .
Speak gently.

Walk softly, March, forbear the bitter blow;
Her feet within a trap, her blood upon the snow,
The four little foxes saw their mother go . . .
Walk softly.

Go lightly, Spring, Oh, give them no alarm;
When I covered them with boughs to shelter them from
harm,
The thin blue foxes suckled at my arm . . .
Go lightly.

Step softly, March, with your rampant hurricane;
Nuzzling one another, and whimpering with pain,
The new little foxes are shivering in the rain . . .
Step softly.

—LEW SARETT

The Road Not Taken

Two roads diverged in a yellow wood,
And sorry I could not travel both
And be one traveler, long I stood
And looked down one as far as I could
To where it bent in the undergrowth;

Then took the other, as just as fair,
And having perhaps the better claim,
Because it was grassy and wanted wear;
Though as for that the passing there
Had worn them really about the same,

And both that morning equally lay
In leaves no step had trodden black.
Oh, I kept the first for another day!
Yet knowing how way leads on to way,
I doubted if I should ever come back.

I shall be telling this with a sigh
Somewhere ages and ages hence:
Two roads diverged in a wood, and I—
I took the one less traveled by,
And that has made all the difference.

—ROBERT FROST

Crabbèd Age and Youth

Crabbèd age and youth cannot live together:
Youth is full of pleasance, age is full of care;
Youth like summer morn, age like winter weather;
Youth like summer brave, age like winter bare.
Youth is full of sport, age's breath is short;
    Youth is nimble, age is lame;
Youth is hot and bold, age is weak and cold;
    Youth is wild, and age is tame.
Age, I do abhor thee; youth, I do adore thee;

O, my love, my love is young!
Age, I do defy thee: O, sweet shepherd, hie thee,
For methinks thou stay'st too long.
—WILLIAM SHAKESPEARE

John Henry

John Henry told his Captain,
"Well, a man ain't nothin' but a man,
And before I let that steam drill beat me down,
I'll die with a hammer in my hand,
I'll die with a hammer in my hand."

Well, the Captain says to John Henry,
"Gonna bring that steam drill around,
Gonna take that steam drill out on the job,
Gonna whop that steel on down,
Gonna whop that steel on down."

John Henry had a little woman,
And her name was Polly Ann,
When John Henry took sick and couldn't work one day,
Polly Ann drove steel like a man,
Polly Ann drove steel like a man.

John Henry said to his shaker,
"Shaker, why don't you sing?
I'm throwin' twelve pounds from my hips on down,
Just listen to that cold steel ring,
Just listen to that cold steel ring."

Well, the Captain says to John Henry,
"I believe this mountain's cavin' in."
John Henry said to the Captain,
" 'Tain't nothin' but my hammer suckin' wind,
'Tain't nothin' but my hammer suckin' wind."

The man that invented the steam drill
Thought that he was mighty fine;
John Henry made his fourteen feet,

While the steam drill it made only nine,
While the steam drill it made only nine.

John Henry, O John Henry,
Blood am runnin' red,
Falls right down his hammer to the ground,
Says, "I've beat him to the bottom but I'm dead."
Says, "I've beat him to the bottom but I'm dead."

John Henry had a little woman,
And the dress she wore was red,
She said, "I'm goin' down the railroad track,
I'm goin' where John Henry fell dead.
I'm goin' where John Henry fell dead."

They took John Henry to the buryin' ground,
And they buried him in the sand;
And every locomotive come roarin' round
Says, "There lies a steel-drivin' man."
Says, "There lies a steel-drivin' man."

—Anonymous

O Captain! My Captain!

A TRIBUTE TO ABRAHAM LINCOLN

O Captain! my Captain! our fearful trip is done,
The ship has weather'd every rack, the prize we sought is
    won,
The port is near, the bells I hear, the people all exulting,
While follow eyes the steady keel, the vessel grim and
    daring;
        But O heart! heart! heart!
          O the bleeding drops of red,
            Where on the deck my Captain lies,
              Fallen cold and dead.

O Captain! my Captain! rise up and hear the bells;
Rise up—for you the flag is flung—for you the bugle trills,
For you bouquets and ribbon'd wreaths—for you the shores
    a-crowding,

For you they call, the swaying mass, their eager faces
        turning;
        Here Captain! dear father!
          The arm beneath your head!
            It is some dream that on the deck,
              You've fallen cold and dead.

My Captain does not answer, his lips are pale and still,
My father does not feel my arm, he has no pulse nor will,
The ship is anchor'd safe and sound, its voyage closed and
        done,
From fearful trip the victor ship comes in with object won;
        Exult O shores, and ring O bells!
          But I with mournful tread,
            Walk the deck my Captain lies,
              Fallen cold and dead.

                    —WALT WHITMAN

Abraham Lincoln Walks at Midnight

It is portentous, and a thing of state
    That here at midnight, in our little town
A mourning figure walks, and will not rest
    Near the old courthouse pacing up and down,

Or by his homestead, or the shadowed yards
    He lingers where his children used to play,
Or through the market, on the well-worn stones
    He stalks until the dawn-stars burn away.

A bronzed, lank man! His suit of ancient black,
    A famous high-top-hat and plain worn shawl
Make him the quaint great figure that men love,
    The prairie-lawyer, master of us all.

He cannot sleep upon his hillside now.
    He is among us, as in times before!
And we who toss and lie awake for long
    Breathe deep, and start, to see him pass the door.

His head is bowed. He thinks on men and kings.
    Yea, when the sick world cries, how can he sleep?
Too many peasants fight, they know not why,
    Too many homesteads in black terror weep.

The sins of all the war lords burn his heart.
    He sees the dreadnaughts scouring every main.
He carries on his shawl-wrapt shoulders now
    The bitterness, the folly and the pain.

He cannot rest until a spirit-dawn
    Shall come;—the shining hope of Europe free;
The league of sober folk, the Workers' Earth
    Bringing long peace to Cornland, Alp, and Sea.

It breaks his heart that kings must murder still,
    That all his hours of travail here for men
Seem yet in vain. And who will bring white peace
    That he may sleep upon his hill again?
                                        —VACHEL LINDSAY

Dulce et Decorum Est

Bent double, like old beggars under sacks,
Knock-kneed, coughing like hags, we cursed through sludge,
Till on the haunting flares we turned our backs,
And towards our distant rest began to trudge.
Men marched asleep. Many had lost their boots,
But limped on, blood-shod. All went lame, all blind;
Drunk with fatigue; deaf even to the hoots
Of gas shells dropping softly behind.

Gas! Gas! Quick, boys!—An ecstasy of fumbling,
Fitting the clumsy helmets just in time,
But someone still was yelling out and stumbling
And flound'ring like a man in fire or lime.
Dim through the misty panes and thick green light,
As under a green sea, I saw him drowning.

In all my dreams before my helpless sight
He plunges at me, guttering, choking, drowning.

If in some smothering dreams, you too could pace
Behind the wagon that we flung him in,
And watch the white eyes writhing in his face,
His hanging face, like a devil's sick of sin;
If you could hear, at every jolt, the blood
Come gargling from the froth-corrupted lungs,
Bitten as the cud
Of vile, incurable sores on innocent tongues,
My friend, you would not tell with such high zest
To children ardent for some desperate glory,
The old Lie: Dulce et decorum est
Pro patria mori.*

—WILFRED OWEN

* It is sweet and fitting to die for one's country.

High Flight

Oh, I have slipped the surly bonds of earth,
And danced the skies on laughter-silvered wings;
Sunward I've climbed and joined the tumbling mirth
Of sun-split clouds—and done a hundred things
You have not dreamed of—wheeled and soared and swung
High in the sunlit silence. Hov'ring there,
I've chased the shouting wing along and flung
My eager craft through footless halls of air.
Up, up the long delirious, burning blue
I've topped the wind-swept heights with easy grace,
Where never lark, or even eagle, flew:
And, while with silent, lifting mind I've trod
The high untrespassed sanctity of space,
Put out my hand, and touched the face of God.

—JOHN GILLESPIE MAGEE

I Did Not Lose My Heart in Summer's Even

I did not lose my heart in summer's even,
  When roses to the moonrise burst apart:
When plumes were under heel and lead was flying,
  In blood and smoke and flame I lost my heart.

I lost it to a soldier and a foeman,
  A chap that did not kill me, but he tried;
That took the saber straight and took it striking
  And laughed and kissed his hand to me and died.
                                    —A. E. Housman

Fog

The fog comes
on little cat feet.
It sits looking
over harbor and city
on silent haunches
and then moves on.
        —Carl Sandburg

Gunga Din

You may talk o' gin an' beer
When you're quartered safe out 'ere,
An' you're sent to penny-fights an' Aldershot it;
But when it comes to slaughter
You will do your work on water,
An' you'll lick the bloomin' boots of 'im that's got it.
Now in Injia's sunny clime,

Where I used to spend my time
A-servin' of 'Er Majesty the Queen,
Of all them black-faced crew
The finest man I knew
Was our regimental *bhisti*, Gunga Din.

> It was "Din! Din! Din!
> You limping lump o' brick-dust, Gunga Din!
> Hi! *slippy hitherao!*
> Water, get it! *Panee lao!*
> You squidgy-nosed old idol, Gunga Din!"

The uniform 'e wore
Was nothin' much before,
An' rather less than 'arf o' that be'ind,
For a twisty piece o' rag
An' a goatskin water-bag
Was all the field-equipment 'e could find.
When the sweatin' troop-train lay
In a sidin' through the day,
Where the 'eat would make your bloomin' eyebrows crawl,
We shouted "*Harry By!*"
Till our throats were bricky-dry,
Then we wopped 'im 'cause 'e couldn't serve us all.

> It was "Din! Din! Din!
> You 'eathen, where the mischief 'ave you been?
> You put some *juldee* in it,
> Or I'll *marrow* you this minute,
> If you don't fill up my helmet, Gunga Din!"

'E would dot an' carry one
Till the longest day was done,
An' 'e didn't seem to know the use o' fear.
If we charged or broke or cut,
You could bet your bloomin' nut,
'E'd be waitin' fifty paces right flank rear. 36344
With 'is *mussick* on 'is back,
'E would skip with our attack,
An' watch us till the bugles made "Retire."
An' for all 'is dirty 'ide,
'E was white, clear white, inside
When 'e went to tend the wounded under fire!

It was "Din! Din! Din!"
With the bullets kickin' dust-spots on the green.
When the cartridges ran out,
You could 'ear the front-files shout:
"Hi! ammunition-mules an' Gunga Din!"

I sha'n't forgit the night
When I dropped be'ind the fight
With a bullet where my belt-plate should 'a' been.
I was chokin' mad with thirst,
An' the man that spied me first
Was our good old grinnin', gruntin' Gunga Din.
'E lifted up my 'ead,
An' 'e plugged me where I bled,
An' 'e guv me 'arf-a-pint o' water—green;
It was crawlin' an' it stunk,
But of all the drinks I've drunk,
I'm gratefulest to one from Gunga Din.

    It was "Din! Din! Din!
    'Ere's a beggar with a bullet through 'is spleen;
    'E's chawin' up the ground an' 'e's kickin' all around:
    For Gawd's sake, git the water, Gunga Din!"

'E carried me away
To where a *dooli* lay,
An' a bullet come an' drilled the beggar clean.
'E put me safe inside,
An' just before 'e died:
"I 'ope you liked your drink," sez Gunga Din.
So I'll meet 'im later on
In the place where 'e is gone—
Where it's always double drill and no canteen;
'E'll be squattin' on the coals
Givin' drink to pore damned souls,
An' I'll get a swig in Hell from Gunga Din!

    Din! Din! Din!
    You Lazarushian-leather Gunga Din!
    Tho' I've belted you an' flayed you,
    By the livin' Gawd that made you,
    You're a better man than I am, Gunga Din!

                  —RUDYARD KIPLING

Renascence

All I could see from where I stood
Was three long mountains and a wood;
I turned and looked another way,
And saw three islands in a bay.
So with my eyes I traced the line
Of the horizon, thin and fine,
Straight around till I was come
Back to where I'd started from;
And all I saw from where I stood
Was three long mountains and a wood.
Over these things I could not see;
These were the things that bounded me;
And I could touch them with my hand,
Almost, I thought, from where I stand.
And all at once things seemed so small
My breath came short, and scarce at all.
But, sure, the sky is big, I said;
Miles and miles above my head;
So here upon my back I'll lie
And look my fill into the sky.
And so I looked, and, after all,
The sky was not so very tall.
The sky, I said, must somewhere stop,
And—sure enough!—I see the top!
The sky, I thought, is not so grand;
I 'most could touch it with my hand!
And, reaching up my hand to try,
I screamed to feel it touch the sky.

I screamed, and—lo—Infinity
Came down and settled over me;
Forced back my scream into my chest,
Bent back my arm upon my breast,
And, pressing of the Undefined
The definition on my mind,
Held up before my eyes a glass
Through which my shrinking sight did pass
Until it seemed I must behold
Immensity made manifold;
Whispered to me a word whose sound
Deafened the air for worlds around,

And brought unmuffled to my ears
The gossiping of friendly spheres,
The creaking of the tented sky,
The ticking of Eternity.

I saw and heard, and knew at last
The How and Why of all things, past,
And present, and forevermore.
The universe, cleft to the core,
Lay open to my probing sense
That, sickening, I would fain pluck thence
But could not,—nay! But needs must suck
At the great wound, and could not pluck
My lips away till I had drawn
All venom out.—Ah, fearful pawn!
For my omniscience I paid toll
In infinite remorse of soul.
All sin was of my sinning, all
Atoning mine, and mine the gall
Of all regret. Mine was the weight
Of every brooded wrong, the hate
That stood behind each envious thrust,
Mine every greed, mine every lust.
And all the while for every grief,
Each suffering, I craved relief
With individual desire,—
Craved all in vain! And felt fierce fire
About a thousand people crawl;
Perished with each,—then mourned for all!
A man was starving in Capri;
He moved his eyes and looked at me;
I felt his gaze, I heard his moan,
And knew his hunger as my own.
I saw at sea a great fog-bank
Between two ships that struck and sank;
A thousand screams the heavens smote;
And every scream tore through my throat;
No hurt I did not feel, no death
That was not mine; mine each last breath
That, crying, met an answering cry
From the compassion that was I.
All suffering mine, and mine its rod;
Mine, pity like the pity of God.
Ah, awful weight! Infinity

Pressed down upon the finite me!
My anguished spirit, like a bird,
Beating against my lips I heard;
Yet lay the weight so close about
There was no room for it without.
And so beneath the weight lay I
And suffered death, but could not die.

Long had I lain thus, craving death,
When quietly the earth beneath
Gave way, and inch by inch, so great
At last had grown the crushing weight,
Into the earth I sank till I
Full six feet under ground did lie,
And sank no more,—there is no weight
Can follow here, however great.
From off my breast I felt it roll,
And as it went my tortured soul
Burst forth and fled in such a gust
That all about me swirled the dust.

Deep in the earth I rested now;
Cool is its hand upon the brow
And soft its breast beneath the head
Of one who is so gladly dead.
And all at once, and over all,
The pitying rain began to fall.
I lay and heard each pattering hoof
Upon my lowly, thatchèd roof.
And seemed to love the sound far more
Than ever I had done before.
For rain it hath a friendly sound
To one who's six feet underground;
And scarce the friendly voice or face:
A grave is such a quiet place.

The rain, I said, is kind to come
And speak to me in my new home.
I would I were alive again
To kiss the fingers of the rain,
To drink into my eyes the shine
Of every slanting silver line,
To catch the freshened, fragrant breeze
From drenched and dripping appletrees.

For soon the shower will be done,
And then the broad face of the sun
Will laugh above the rain-soaked earth
Until the world with answering mirth
Shakes joyously, and each round drop
Rolls, twinkling, from its grass-blade top.
How can I bear it; buried here,
While overhead the sky grows clear
And blue again after the storm?
O, multicolored, multiform,
Belovèd beauty over me,
That I shall never, never see
Again! Spring-silver, autumn-gold,
That I shall never more behold!
Sleeping your myriad magics through,
Close-sepulchered away from you!
O God, I cried, give me new birth,
And put me back upon the earth!
Upset each cloud's gigantic gourd
And let the heavy rain, down-poured
In one big torrent, set me free,
Washing my grave away from me!

I ceased; and, through the breathless hush
That answered me, the far-off rush
Of herald wings came whispering
Like music down the vibrant string
Of my ascending prayer, and—crash!
Before the wild wind's whistling lash
The startled storm-clouds reared on high
And plunged in terror down the sky,
And the big rain in one black wave
Fell from the sky and struck my grave.

I know not how such things can be,
I only know there came to me
A fragrance such as never clings
To aught save happy living things;
A sound as of some joyous elf
Singing sweet songs to please himself,
And, through and over everything,
A sense of glad awakening.
The grass, a tiptoe at my ear,
Whispering to me I could hear;

I felt the rain's cool finger tips
Brushed tenderly across my lips,
Laid gently on my sealèd sight,
And all at once the heavy night
Fell from my eyes and I could see,—
A drenched and dripping appletree,
A last long line of silver rain,
A sky grown clear and blue again.
And as I looked a quickening gust
Of wind blew up to me and thrust
Into my face a miracle
Of orchard-breath, and with the smell,—
I know not how such things can be!—
I breathed my soul back into me.

Ah! Up then from the ground sprang I
And hailed the earth with such a cry
As is not heard save from a man
Who has been dead and lives again.
About the trees my arms I wound;
Like one gone mad I hugged the ground;
I raised my quivering arms on high;
I laughed and laughed into the sky,
Till at my throat a strangling sob
Caught fiercely, and a great heartthrob
Sent instant tears into my eyes;
O God, I cried, no dark disguise
Can e'er hereafter hide from me
Thy radiant identity!
Thou canst not move across the grass
But my quick eyes will see Thee pass,
Nor speak, however silently,
But my hushed voice will answer Thee.
I know the path that tells Thy way
Through the cool eve of every day;
God, I can push the grass apart
And lay my finger on Thy heart!

The world stands out on either side
No wider than the heart is wide;
Above the world is stretched the sky,—
No higher than the soul is high.
The heart can push the sea and land
Farther away on either hand;

The soul can split the sky in two,
And let the face of God shine through.
But East and West will pinch the heart
That cannot keep them pushed apart;
And he whose soul is flat—the sky
Will cave in on him by and by.

—Edna St. Vincent Millay

If

If you can keep your head when all about you
    Are losing theirs and blaming it on you,
If you can trust yourself when all men doubt you,
    But make allowance for their doubting too;
If you can wait and not be tired by waiting,
    Or being lied about, don't deal in lies,
Or being hated don't give way to hating,
    And yet don't look too good, nor talk too wise:

If you can dream—and not make dreams your master;
    If you can think—and not make thoughts your aim,
If you can meet with Triumph and Disaster
    And treat those two impostors just the same;
If you can bear to hear the truth you've spoken
    Twisted by knaves to make a trap for fools,
Or watch the things you gave your life to, broken,
    And stoop and build 'em up with worn-out tools:

If you can make one heap of all your winnings;
    And risk it on one turn of pitch-and-toss,
And lose, and start again at your beginnings
    And never breathe a word about your loss;
If you can force your heart and nerve and sinew
    To serve your turn long after they are gone
And so hold on when there is nothing in you
    Except the Will which says to them: "Hold on!"

If you can talk with crowds and keep your virtue,
    Or walk with Kings—nor lose the common touch,

If neither foes nor loving friends can hurt you,
  If all men count with you, but none too much;
If you can fill the unforgiving minute
  With sixty seconds' worth of distance run,
Yours is the Earth and everything that's in it,
    And—which is more—you'll be a Man, my son!
                              —RUDYARD KIPLING

Little Boy Blue

The little toy dog is covered with dust,
  But sturdy and stanch he stands;
And the little toy soldier is red with rust,
  And his musket molds in his hands.
Time was when the little toy dog was new
  And the soldier was passing fair,
And that was the time when our Little Boy Blue
  Kissed them and put them there.

"Now, don't you go till I come," he said,
  "And don't you make any noise!"
So toddling off to his trundle-bed
  He dreamed of the pretty toys.
And as he was dreaming, an angel song
  Awakened our Little Boy Blue—
Oh, the years are many, the years are long,
  But the little toy friends are true.

Ay, faithful to Little Boy Blue they stand,
  Each in the same old place,
Awaiting the touch of a little hand,
  And the smile of a little face.
And they wonder, as waiting the long years through,
  In the dust of that little chair,
What has become of our Little Boy Blue
  Since he kissed them and put them there.
                              —EUGENE FIELD

My Papa's Waltz

The whiskey on your breath
Could make a small boy dizzy;
But I hung on like death:
Such waltzing was not easy.

We romped until the pans
Slid from the kitchen shelf;
My mother's countenance
Could not unfrown itself.

The hand that held my wrist
Was battered on one knuckle;
At every step you missed
My right ear scraped a buckle.

You beat time on my head
With a palm caked hard by dirt,
Then waltzed me off to bed
Still clinging to your shirt.

—THEODORE ROETHKE

Recuerdo

We were very tired, we were very merry—
We had gone back and forth all night on the ferry.
It was bare and bright, and smelled like a stable—
But we looked into a fire, and we leaned across a table,
We lay on a hilltop underneath the moon;
And the whistles kept blowing, and the dawn came soon.

We were very tired, we were very merry—
We had gone back and forth all night on the ferry;
And you ate an apple, and I ate a pear,
From a dozen of each we had bought somewhere;
And the sky went wan, and the wind came cold,
And the sun rose dripping, a bucketful of gold.

We were very tired, we were very merry,
We had gone back and forth all night on the ferry.
We hailed, "Good-morrow, mother!" to a shawl-covered
head,
And bought a morning paper which neither of us read;
And she wept, "God bless you!" for the apples and the
pears,
And we gave her all our money but our subway fares.

—EDNA ST. VINCENT MILLAY

The Raven

Once upon a midnight dreary, while I pondered, weak and
weary,
Over many a quaint and curious volume of forgotten lore,
While I nodded, nearly napping, suddenly there came a
tapping,
As of someone gently rapping, rapping at my chamber
door.
" 'Tis some visitor," I muttered, "tapping at my chamber
door—
        Only this and nothing more."

Ah, distinctly I remember it was in the bleak December,
And each separate dying ember wrought its ghost upon the
floor.
Eagerly I wished the morrow; vainly I had sought to
borrow
From my books surcease of sorrow—sorrow for the lost
Lenore,
For the rare and radiant maiden whom the angels name
Lenore—
        Nameless *here* for evermore.

And the silken, sad, uncertain rustling of each purple
curtain
Thrilled me—filled me with fantastic terrors never felt
before;
So that now, to still the beating of my heart, I stood
repeating,

" 'Tis some visitor entreating entrance at my chamber
        door—
Some late visitor entreating entrance at my chamber
        door—
            This it is and nothing more."

Presently my soul grew stronger: hesitating then no longer,
"Sir," said I, "or Madam, truly your forgiveness I implore;
But the fact is I was napping, and so gently you came
        rapping,
And so faintly you came tapping, tapping at my chamber
        door,
That I scarce was sure I heard you"—here I opened wide
        the door—
            Darkness there and nothing more.

Deep into that darkness peering, long I stood there, won-
        dering, fearing,
Doubting, dreaming dreams no mortal ever dared to dream
        before;
But the silence was unbroken, and the stillness gave no
        token,
And the only word there spoken was the whispered word
        "Lenore!"
This I whispered, and an echo murmured back the word
        "Lenore!"
            Merely this and nothing more.

Back into the chamber turning, all my soul within me
        burning,
Soon again I heard a tapping, somewhat louder than
        before.
"Surely," said I, "surely that is something at my window
        lattice;
Let me see, then, what thereat is, and this mystery ex-
        plore,—
Let my heart be still a moment and this mystery explore—
            'Tis the wind and nothing more."

Open here I flung the shutter, when, with many a flirt
        and flutter,
In there stepped a stately Raven of the saintly days of yore.
Not the least obeisance made he, not a minute stopped or
        stayed he,

But with mien of lord or lady perched above my chamber
    door—
Perched upon a bust of Pallas just above my chamber
    door—
        Perched and sat, and nothing more.

Then, this ebony bird beguiling my sad fancy into smiling
By the grave and stern decorum of the countenance it
    wore,
"Though thy crest be shorn and shaven, thou," I said,
    "art sure no craven,
Ghastly, grim, and ancient Raven, wandering from the
    nightly shore:
Tell me what thy lordly name is on the night's Plutonian
    shore!"
        Quoth the Raven, "Nevermore."

Much I marveled this ungainly fowl to hear discourse so
    plainly,
Though its answer little meaning, little relevancy bore;
For we cannot help agreeing that no living human being
Ever yet was blessed with seeing bird above his chamber
    door—
Bird or beast upon the sculptured bust above his chamber
    door—
        With such name as "Nevermore."

But the Raven, sitting lonely on the placid bust, spoke only
That one word, as if his soul in that one word he did out-
    pour.
Nothing further then he uttered, not a feather then he
    fluttered;
Till I scarcely more than muttered, "Other friends have
    flown before:
On the morrow *he* will leave me, as my hopes have flown
    before."
        Then the bird said, "Nevermore."

Startled at the stillness broken by reply so aptly spoken,
"Doubtless," said I, "what it utters is its only stock and
    store,
Caught from some unhappy master whom unmerciful
    Disaster

39

Followed fast and followed faster till his songs one burden
  bore,
Till the dirges of his hope that melancholy burden bore
  Of 'Never—nevermore.' "

But the Raven still beguiling all my sad soul into smiling,
Straight I wheeled a cushioned seat in front of bird and
  bust and door;
Then, upon the velvet sinking, I betook myself to linking
Fancy unto fancy, thinking what this ominous bird of yore,
What this grim, ungainly, ghastly, gaunt, and ominous
  bird of yore
  Meant in croaking "Nevermore."

This I sat engaged in guessing, but no syllable expressing
To the fowl, whose fiery eyes now burned into my bosom's
  core;
This and more I sat divining, with my head at ease re-
  clining
On the cushion's velvet lining that the lamplight gloated
  o'er,
But whose velvet violet lining with the lamplight gloat-
  ing o'er,
  She shall press, ah, nevermore!

Then, methought, the air grew denser, perfumed from an
  unseen censer
Swung by seraphim whose footfalls tinkled on the tufted
  floor.
"Wretch," I cried, "thy God hath lent thee—by these
  angels he hath sent thee
Respite—respite and nepenthe from thy memories of
  Lenore!
Quaff, oh quaff this kind nepenthe, and forget this lost
  Lenore!"
  Quoth the Raven, "Nevermore."

"Prophet!" said I, "thing of evil! prophet still, if bird or
  devil!
Whether Tempter sent, or whether tempest tossed thee
  here ashore,
Desolate yet all undaunted, on this desert land en-
  chanted—

On this home by Horror haunted—tell me truly, I implore:
Is there—*is* there balm in Gilead?—tell me—tell me, I implore!"
        Quoth the Raven, "Nevermore."

"Prophet!" said I, "thing of evil—prophet still, if bird or devil!
By that Heaven that bends above us, by that God we both adore,
Tell this soul with sorrow laden if, within the distant Aidenn,
It shall clasp a sainted maiden whom the angels name Lenore:
Clasp a rare and radiant maiden whom the angels name Lenore!"
        Quoth the Raven, "Nevermore."

"Be that word our sign of parting, bird or fiend!" I shrieked, upstarting:
"Get thee back into the tempest and the Night's Plutonian shore!
Leave no black plume as a token of that lie thy soul hath spoken!
Leave my loneliness unbroken! quit the bust above my door!
Take thy beak from out my heart, and take thy form from off my door!"
        Quoth the Raven, "Nevermore."

And the Raven, never flitting, still is sitting, still is sitting
On the pallid bust of Pallas just above my chamber door;
And his eyes have all the seeming of a demon's that is dreaming,
And the lamplight o'er him streaming throws his shadow on the floor;
And my soul from out that shadow that lies floating on the floor
        Shall be lifted—nevermore!
                —EDGAR ALLAN POE

More About People

When people aren't asking questions
They're making suggestions
And when they're not doing one of those
They're either looking over your shoulder or stepping on
      your toes
And then as if that weren't enough to annoy you
They employ you.
Anybody at leisure
Incurs everybody's displeasure.
It seems to be very irking
To people at work to see other people not working,
So they tell you that work is wonderful medicine,
Just look at Firestone and Ford and Edison,
And then they lecture you till they're out of breath or
      something
And then if you don't succumb they starve you to death or
      something.
All of which results in a nasty quirk:
That if you don't want to work you have to work to earn
      enough money so that you won't have to work.

              —OGDEN NASH

in Just—

    in Just—
    spring   when the world is mud-
    luscious the little
    lame balloonman

    whistles   far   and wee

    and eddieandbill come
    running from marbles and
    piracies and it's
    spring

    When the world is puddle-wonderful

the queer
old balloonman whistles
far   and   wee
and bettyandisbel come dancing

from hop-scotch and jump-rope and

it's
spring
and
    the

      goat-footed

balloonman   whistles
far
and
wee

—E. E. CUMMINGS

To Helen

Helen, thy beauty is to me
  Like those Nicèan barks of yore
That gently, o'er a perfumed sea,
  The weary, way-worn wanderer bore
  To his own native shore.

On desperate seas long wont to roam,
  Thy hyacinth hair, thy classic face,
Thy Naiad airs have brought me home
  To the glory that was Greece,
And the grandeur that was Rome.

Lo, in yon brilliant window niche
  How statuelike I see thee stand,
  The agate lamp within thy hand,
Ah! Psyche, from the regions which
  Are Holy Land!

—EDGAR ALLAN POE

Upon Westminster Bridge

Earth has not anything to show more fair:
Dull would he be of soul who could pass by
A sight so touching in its majesty:
This City now doth, like a garment, wear
The beauty of the morning; silent, bare,
Ships, towers, domes, theatres and temples lie
Open unto the fields, and to the sky;
All bright and glittering in the smokeless air.
Never did sun more beautifully steep
In his first splendor, valley, rock, or hill;
Ne'er saw I, never felt, a calm so deep!
The river glideth at his own sweet will:
Dear God! the very houses seem asleep;
And all that mighty heart is lying still!

—WILLIAM WORDSWORTH

The Little Black Boy

My mother bore me in the southern wild,
And I am black, but O! my soul is white;
White as an angel is the English child,
But I am black, as if bereav'd of light.

My mother taught me underneath a tree,
And, sitting down before the heat of day,
She took me on her lap and kissèd me,
And, pointing to the east, began to say:

"Look on the rising sun,—there God does live,
And gives His light, and gives His heat away;
And flowers and trees and beasts and men receive
Comfort in morning, joy in the noonday.

"And we are put on earth a little space,
That we may learn to bear the beams of love;
And these black bodies and this sunburnt face
Are but a cloud, and like a shady grove.

44

"For when our souls have learn'd the heat to bear,
The cloud will vanish; we shall hear His voice,
Saying: 'Come out from the grove, My love and care,
And round My golden tent like lambs rejoice.'"

Thus did my mother say, and kissèd me;
And thus I say to little English boy.
When I from black and he from white cloud free,
And round the tent of God like lambs we joy,

I'll shade him from the heat, till he can bear
To lean in joy upon our Father's knee;
And then I'll stand and stroke his silver hair,
And be like him, and he will then love me.

—WILLIAM BLAKE

Success Is Counted Sweetest

Success is counted sweetest
By those who ne'er succeed.
To comprehend a nectar
Requires sorest need.

Not one of all the purple host
Who took the flag today
Can tell the definition,
So clear, of victory,

As he, defeated, dying,
On whose forbidden ear
The distant strains of triumph
Break, agonized and clear.

—EMILY DICKINSON

My Dreams Are of a Field Afar

My dreams are of a field afar
　　And blood and smoke and shot.
There in their graves my comrades are,
　　In my grave I am not.
I too was taught the trade of man
　　And spelt the lesson plain;
But they, when I forgot and ran,
　　Remembered and remain.

　　　　　　　　　—A. E. Housman

I Have a Rendezvous with Death

I have a rendezvous with Death
At some disputed barricade,
When Spring comes back with rustling shade
And appleblossoms fill the air—
I have a rendezvous with Death
When Spring brings back blue days and fair.

It may be he shall take my hand
And lead me into his dark land
And close my eyes and quench my breath—
It may be I shall pass him still.
I have a rendezvous with Death
On some scarred slope of battered hill,
When Spring comes round again this year
And the first meadow flowers appear.

God knows 'twere better to be deep
Pillowed in silk and scented down,
Where Love throbs out in blissful sleep,
Pulse nigh to pulse, and breath to breath,
Where hushed awakenings are dear . . .
But I've a rendezvous with Death
At midnight in some flaming town,
When Spring trips north again this year,

And I to my pledged word am true,
I shall not fail that rendezvous.

—ALAN SEEGER

Trees

I think that I shall never see
A poem lovely as a tree.

A tree whose hungry mouth is prest
Against the earth's sweet flowing breast;

A tree that looks at God all day
And lifts her leafy arms to pray;

A tree that may in summer wear
A nest of robins in her hair;

Upon whose bosom snow has lain;
Who intimately lives with rain.

Poems are made by fools like me,
But only God can make a tree.

—JOYCE KILMER

The World Is Too Much with Us

The world is too much with us; late and soon,
Getting and spending, we lay waste our powers:
Little we see in Nature that is ours;
We have given our hearts away, a sordid boon!
The Sea that bares her bosom to the moon;
The winds that will be howling at all hours,
And are upgathered now like sleeping flowers;
For this, for everything, we are out of tune;
It moves us not.—Great God! I'd rather be

A Pagan, suckled in a creed outworn,
So might I, standing on this pleasant lea,
Have glimpses that would make me less forlorn;
Have sight of Proteus rising from the sea;
Or hear old Triton blow his wreathèd horn.

—WILLIAM WORDSWORTH

Leisure

What is this life if, full of care,
We have no time to stand and stare.

No time to stand beneath the boughs
And stare as long as sheep or cows.

No time to see, when woods we pass,
Where squirrels hide their nuts in grass.

No time to see, in broad daylight,
Streams full of stars, like skies at night.

No time to turn at Beauty's glance,
And watch her feet, how they can dance.

No time to wait till her mouth can
Enrich that smile her eyes began.

A poor life this if, full of care,
We have no time to stand and stare.

—W. H. DAVIES

Patterns

I walk down the garden paths,
And all the daffodils
Are blowing, and the bright blue squills.

I walk down the patterned garden paths
In my stiff, brocaded gown.
With my powdered hair and jeweled fan,
I too am a rare
Pattern. As I wander down
The garden paths.
My dress is richly figured,
And the train
Makes a pink and silver stain
On the gravel, and the thrift
Of the borders.
Just a plate of current fashion,
Tripping by in high-heeled, ribboned shoes.
Not a softness anywhere about me,
Only whalebone and brocade.
And I sink on a seat in the shade
Of a lime tree. For my passion
Wars against the stiff brocade.
The daffodils and squills
Flutter in the breeze
As they please.
And I weep;
For the lime tree is in blossom
And one small flower has dropped upon my bosom.

And the plashing of waterdrops
In the marble fountain
Comes down the garden paths.
The dripping never stops.
Underneath my stiffened gown
Is the softness of a woman bathing in a marble basin,
A basin in the midst of hedges grown
So thick, she cannot see her lover hiding.
But she guesses he is near,
And the sliding of the water
Seems the stroking of a dear
Hand upon her.
What is Summer in a fine brocaded gown!
I should like to see it lying in a heap upon the ground.
All the pink and silver crumpled upon the ground.

I would be the pink and silver as I ran along the paths,
And he would stumble after,
Bewildered by my laughter.

I should see the sun flashing from his sword hilt and the
     buckles on his shoes.
I would choose
To lead him in a maze along the patterned paths,
A bright and laughing maze for my heavy-booted lover,
Till he caught me in the shade,
And the buttons of his waistcoat bruised my body as he
     clasped me,
Aching, melting, unafraid.
With the shadows of the leaves and the sundrops,
And the plopping of the waterdrops,
All about us in the open afternoon—
I am very like to swoon
With the weight of this brocade,
For the sun shifts through the shade.

Underneath the fallen blossom
In my bosom
Is a letter I have hid.
It was brought to me this morning by a rider from the
     Duke.
"Madam, we regret to inform you that Lord Hartwell
Died in action Thursday se'nnight."
As I read it in the white, morning sunlight,
The letters squirmed like snakes.
"Any answer, Madam," said my footman.
"No," I told him.
"See that the messenger takes some refreshment.
No, no answer."
And I walked into the garden,
Up and down the patterned paths,
In my stiff, correct brocade.
The blue and yellow flowers stood up proudly in the sun,
Each one.
I stood upright too,
Held rigid to the pattern
By the stiffness of my gown;
Up and down I walked,
Up and down.

In a month he would have been my husband.
In a month, here, underneath this lime,
We would have broke the pattern;
He for me, and I for him,

He as Colonel, I as Lady,
On this shady seat.
He had a whim
That sunlight carried blessing.
And I answered, "It shall be as you have said."
Now he is dead.
In Summer and in Winter I shall walk
Up and down
The patterned garden paths
In my stiff, brocaded gown.
The squills and daffodils
Will give place to pillared roses, and to asters, and to
        snow.
I shall go
Up and down
In my gown.
Gorgeously arrayed,
Boned and stayed.
And the softness of my body will be guarded from embrace
By each button, hook, and lace.
For the man who should loose me is dead,
Fighting with the Duke in Flanders,
In a pattern called a war.
Christ! What are patterns for?

—AMY LOWELL

Kubla Khan

In Xanadu did Kubla Khan
A stately pleasure-dome decree:
Where Alph, the sacred river, ran
    Through caverns measureless to man
        Down to a sunless sea.
So twice five miles of fertile ground
With walls and towers were girdled round:
And here were gardens bright with sinuous rills
Where blossomed many an incense-bearing tree;
And here were forests ancient as the hills,
Enfolding sunny spots of greenery.
But oh! that deep romantic chasm which slanted

51

Down the green hill athwart a cedarn cover!
A savage place! as holy and enchanted
As e'er beneath a waning moon was haunted
By woman wailing for her demon-lover!
And from this chasm, with ceaseless turmoil seething,
As if this earth in fast thick pants were breathing,
A mighty fountain momently was forced;
Amid whose swift half-intermitted burst
Huge fragments vaulted like rebounding hail,
Or chaffy grain beneath the thresher's flail:
And mid these dancing rocks at once and ever
It flung up momently the sacred river.
Five miles meandering with a mazy motion
Through wood and dale the sacred river ran,
Then reached the caverns measureless to man,
And sank in tumult to a lifeless ocean:
And mid this tumult Kubla heard from far
Ancestral voices prophesying war!
The shadow of the dome of pleasure
    Floated midway on the waves;
Where was heard the mingled measure
    From the fountain and the caves.
It was a miracle of rare device,
A sunny pleasure-dome with caves of ice!

    A damsel with a dulcimer
    In a vision once I saw:
    It was an Abyssinian maid,
    And on her dulcimer she play'd,
    Singing of Mount Abora.
    Could I revive within me
    Her symphony and song,
To such a deep delight 'twould win me,
That with music loud and long,
I would build that dome in air,
That sunny dome! those caves of ice!
And all who heard should see them there,
And all should cry, Beware! Beware!
His flashing eyes, his floating hair!
Weave a circle round him thrice,
And close your eyes with holy dread,
For he on honeydew hath fed,
And drunk the milk of Paradise.

—SAMUEL TAYLOR COLERIDGE

The Barefoot Boy

Blessings on thee, little man,
Barefoot boy, with cheek of tan!
With thy turned-up pantaloons,
And thy merry whistled tunes;
With thy red lip, redder still
Kissed by strawberries on the hill;
With the sunshine on thy face,
Through thy torn brim's jaunty grace;
From my heart I give thee joy,—
I was once a barefoot boy!
Prince thou art,—the grown-up man
Only is republican.
Let the million-dollared ride!
Barefoot, trudging at his side,
Thou hast more than he can buy
In the reach of ear and eye,—
Outward sunshine, inward joy:
Blessings on thee, barefoot boy!

Oh for boyhood's painless play,
Sleep that wakes in laughing day,
Health that mocks the doctor's rules,
Knowledge never learned of schools,
Of the wild bee's morning chase,
Of the wild flower's time and place,
Flight of fowl and habitude
Of the tenants of the wood;
How the tortoise bears his shell,
How the woodchuck digs his cell,
And the ground mole sinks his well;
How the robin feeds her young,
How the oriole's nest is hung;
Where the whitest lilies blow,
Where the freshest berries grow,
Where the groundnut trails its vine,
Where the wood grape's clusters shine;
Of the black wasp's cunning way,
Mason of his walls of clay,
And the architectural plans
Of gray hornet artisans!
For, eschewing books and tasks,

53

Nature answers all he asks;
Hand in hand with her he walks,
Face to face with her he talks,
Part and parcel of her joy,—
Blessings on the barefoot boy!

Oh for boyhood's time of June,
Crowding years in one brief moon,
When all things I heard or saw,
Me, their master, waited for.
I was rich in flowers and trees,
Hummingbirds and honeybees;
For my sport the squirrel played,
Plied the snouted mole his spade;
For my taste the blackberry cone
Purpled over hedge and stone;
Laughed the brook for my delight
Through the day and through the night,—
Whispering at the garden wall,
Talked with me from fall to fall;
Mine the sand-rimmed pickerel pond,
Mine the walnut slopes beyond,
Mine, on bending orchard trees,
Apples of Hesperides!
Still as my horizon grew,
Larger grew my riches too;
All the world I saw or knew
Seemed a complex Chinese toy,
Fashioned for a barefoot boy!

Oh for festal dainties spread,
Like my bowl of milk and bread;
Pewter spoon and bowl of wood,
On the doorstone, gray and rude!
O'er me, like a regal tent,
Cloudy-ribbed, the sunset bent,
Purple-curtained, fringed with gold,
Looped in many a wind-swung fold;
While for music came the play
Of pied frogs' orchestra;
And, to light the noisy choir,
Lit the fly his lamp of fire.
I was monarch: pomp and joy
Waited on the barefoot boy!

Cheerily, then, my little man,
Live and laugh, as boyhood can!
Though the flinty slopes be hard,
Stubble-speared the new-mown sward,
Every morn shall lead thee through
Fresh baptisms of the dew;
Every evening from thy feet
Shall the cool wind kiss the heat:
All too soon these feet must hide
In the prison cells of pride,
Lose the freedom of the sod,
Like a colt's for work be shod,
Made to tread the mills of toil,
Up and down in ceaseless moil:
Happy if their track be found
Never on forbidden ground;
Happy if they sink not in
Quick and treacherous sands of sin.
Ah! that thou couldst know thy joy,
Ere it passes, barefoot boy!

—JOHN GREENLEAF WHITTIER

A Red, Red Rose

O my luve is like a red, red rose,
    That's newly sprung in June.
O my luve is like the melodie
    That's sweetly played in tune.

As fair art thou, my bonnie lass,
    So deep in luve am I,
And I will luve thee still, my dear,
    Till a' the seas gang dry.

Till a' the seas gang dry, my dear,
    And the rocks melt wi' the sun!
And I will luve thee still, my dear,
    While the sands o' life shall run.

And fare thee weel, my only luve,
  And fare thee weel awhile!
And I will come again, my luve,
  Tho' it were ten thousand mile!

—ROBERT BURNS

Spring

To what purpose, April, do you return again?
Beauty is not enough.
You can no longer quiet me with redness
Of little leaves opening stickily.
I know what I know.
The sun is hot on my neck as I observe
The spikes of the crocus.
The smell of the earth is good.
It is apparent that there is no death.
But what does that signify?
Not only under ground are the brains of men
Eaten by maggots.
Life in itself
Is nothing,
An empty cup, a flight of uncarpeted stairs.
It is not enough that yearly, down this hill,
April
Comes like an idiot, babbling and strewing flowers.

—EDNA ST. VINCENT MILLAY

To Make a Prairie

To make a prairie it takes a clover and one bee,—
One clover, and a bee
And reverie.
The reverie alone will do
If bees are few.

—EMILY DICKINSON

Belagcholly Days

Chilly Dovebber with his boadigg blast
   Dow cubs add strips the beddow add the lawd,
Eved October's suddy days are past—
   Add Subber's gawd!

I kdow dot what it is to which I cligg
   That stirs to sogg add sorrow, yet I trust
That still I sigg, but as the liddets sigg—
   Because I bust.

Add dow, farewell to roses add to birds,
   To bloobigg fields add tigkligg streablets eke;
Farewell to all articulated words
   I faid would speak.

Farewell, by cherished strolligs od the sward,
   Greed glades add frosty shades, farewell to you;
With sorrowing heart I, wretched add forlord,
   Bid you—achew!

                —Anonymous

Late Fall Once Again

In the dark wood the leaves hiss and glow in the rain.
Soft, succulent vines shiver into purple death,
And mouse and rabbit burrow and build against the bite
   of the cold:
The blood sap returns to the roots.

Who shall salt down this season
That buries its dead with crackling wreaths under the
   moon?
Who shall remember the golden skies scarfing this whirl-
   ing earth?
Who shall watch over the seeds, those brown eyes of the
   spring so soundly sleeping?

Only the wind that blows both hot and cold,
Companion of the sun and just as old.

—Herman M. Ward

I Saw a Man

I saw a man pursuing the horizon;
Round and round they sped.
I was disturbed at this;
I accosted the man.
"It is futile," I said,
"You can never—"

"You lie," he cried,
And ran on.

—Stephen Crane

The Owl-Critic

"Who stuffed that white owl?" No one spoke in the shop,
The barber was busy, and he couldn't stop;
The customers, waiting their turns, were all reading
The *Daily*, the *Herald*, the *Post*, little heeding
The young man who blurted out such a blunt question;
Not one raised a head, or even made a suggestion;
    And the barber kept on shaving.

"Don't you see, Mr. Brown,"
Cried the youth, with a frown,
"How wrong the whole thing is,
How preposterous each wing is,
How flattened the head is, how jammed down the neck
    is—
In short, the whole owl, what an ignorant wreck 'tis!
I make no apology;
I've learned owl-eology,

I've passed days and nights in a hundred collections,
And cannot be blinded to any deflections
Arising from unskillful fingers that fail
To stuff a bird right, from his beak to his tail.
Mister Brown! Mister Brown!
Do take that bird down,
Or you'll soon be the laughingstock all over town!"
        And the barber kept on shaving.

"I've *studied* owls,
And other night fowls,
And I tell you
What I know to be true;
An owl cannot roost
With his limbs so unloosed;
No owl in this world
Ever had his claws curled,
Ever had his legs slanted,
Ever had his bill canted,
Ever had his neck screwed
Into that attitude.
He can't *do* it, because
'Tis against all bird-laws.
Anatomy teaches,
Ornithology preaches,
An owl has a toe
That *can't* turn out so!
I've made the white owl my study for years,
And to see such a job almost moves me to tears!
Mr. Brown, I'm amazed
You should be so gone crazed
As to put up a bird
In that posture absurd!
To *look* at that owl really brings on a dizziness;
The man who stuffed *him* don't half know his business!"
        And the barber kept on shaving.

"Examine those eyes.
I'm filled with surprise
Taxidermists should pass
Off on you such poor glass;
So unnatural they seem
They'd make Audubon scream,
And John Burroughs laugh

To encounter such chaff.
Do take that bird down;
Have him stuffed again, Brown!"
           And the barber kept on shaving.

"With some sawdust and bark
I could stuff in the dark
An owl better than that.
I could make an old hat
Look more like an owl
Than that horrid fowl,
Stuck up there so stiff like a side of coarse leather.
In fact, about *him* there's not one natural feather."
           And the barber kept on shaving.

Just then, with a wink and a sly normal lurch,
The owl, very gravely, got down from his perch,
Walked around, and regarded his fault-finding critic
(Who thought he was stuffed) with a glance analytic,
And then fairly hooted, as if he would say:
"Your learning's at fault *this* time, anyway;
Don't waste it again on a live bird, I pray.
I'm an owl; you're another. Sir Critic, good day!"
           And the barber kept on shaving.

                   —JAMES THOMAS FIELDS

Hark, Hark

Hark, hark,
The dogs do bark,
The beggars are coming to town;
Some in rags,
And some in jags,
And one in a velvet gown.

                —ANONYMOUS

Let Me Not to the Marriage of True Minds

(SONNET 116)

Let me not to the marriage of true minds
Admit impediments. Love is not love
Which alters when it alteration finds,
Or bends with the remover to remove:
O, no! it is an ever-fixèd mark,
That looks on tempests and is never shaken;
It is the star to every wand'ring bark,
Whose worth's unknown, although his height be taken.
Love's not Time's fool, though rosy lips and cheeks
Within his bending sickle's compass come;
Love alters not with his brief hours and weeks,
But bears it out even to the edge of doom:—
    If this be error and upon me proved,
    I never writ, nor no man ever loved.

            —WILLIAM SHAKESPEARE

Shall I Compare Thee to a Summer's Day?

(SONNET 18)

Shall I compare thee to a summer's day?
Thou art more lovely and more temperate.
Rough winds do shake the darling buds of May,
And summer's lease hath all too short a date:
Sometimes too hot the eye of heaven shines,
And often is his gold complexion dimmed:
And every fair from fair sometime declines,
By chance, or nature's changing course, untrimmed:
But thy eternal summer shall not fade
Nor lose possession of that fair thou owest;
Nor shall Death brag thou wanderest in his shade
When in eternal lines to time thou growest.
    So long as men can breathe or eyes can see
    So long lives this, and this gives life to thee.

            —WILLIAM SHAKESPEARE

Afternoon on a Hill

I will be the gladdest thing
    Under the sun!
I will touch a hundred flowers
  And not pick one.

I will look at cliffs and clouds
    With quiet eyes,
Watch the wind bow down the grass,
    And the grass rise.

And when lights begin to show
    Up from the town,
I will mark which must be mine,
    And then start down!

      —Edna St. Vincent Millay

Velvet Shoes

Let us walk in the white snow
    In a soundless space;
With footsteps quiet and slow,
    At a tranquil pace,
    Under veils of white lace.

I shall go shod in silk,
    And you in wool,
White as a white cow's milk,
    More beautiful
    Than the breast of a gull.

We shall walk through the still town
    In a windless peace;
We shall step upon white down,
    Upon silver fleece,
    Upon softer than these.

We shall walk in velvet shoes:
    Wherever we go
Silence will fall like dews
    On white silence below.
    We shall walk in the snow.

—ELINOR WYLIE

Song to Celia

Drink to me only with thine eyes,
    And I will pledge with mine;
Or leave a kiss but in the cup,
    And I'll not look for wine.
The thirst that from the soul doth rise
    Doth ask a drink divine;
But might I of Jove's nectar sup,
    I would not change for thine.

I sent thee late a rosy wreath,
    Not so much honoring thee
As giving it a hope, that there
    It could not withered be.
But thou thereon didst only breathe,
    And sent'st it back to me;
Since when it grows, and smells, I swear,
    Not of itself, but thee.

—BEN JONSON

Chicago

Hog Butcher for the World,
Tool Maker, Stacker of Wheat,
Player with Railroads and the Nation's Freight Handler;
Stormy, husky, brawling,
City of the Big Shoulders:

They tell me you are wicked, and I believe them; for I have seen your painted women under the gas lamps luring the farm boys.

And they tell me you are crooked, and I answer: Yes, it is true I have seen the gunman kill and go free to kill again.

And they tell me you are brutal, and my reply is: On the faces of women and children I have seen the marks of wanton hunger.

And having answered so I turn once more to those who sneer at this my city, and I give them back the sneer and say to them:

Come and show me another city with lifted head singing so proud to be alive and coarse and strong and cunning.

Flinging magnetic curses amid the toil of piling job on job, here is a tall bold slugger set vivid against the little soft cities;

Fierce as a dog with tongue lapping for action, cunning as a savage pitted against the wilderness,
    Bareheaded,
    Shoveling,
    Wrecking,
    Planning,
    Building, breaking, rebuilding,

Under the smoke, dust all over his mouth, laughing with white teeth,

Under the terrible burden of destiny laughing as a young man laughs,

Laughing even as an ignorant fighter laughs who has never lost a battle,

Bragging and laughing that under his wrist is the pulse, and under his ribs the heart of the people,
    Laughing!

Laughing the stormy, husky, brawling laughter of youth; half-naked, sweating, proud to be Hog Butcher, Tool Maker, Stacker of Wheat, Player with Railroads, and Freight Handler to the Nation.

—Carl Sandburg

The Rubáiyát of Omar Khayyám

Wake! For the Sun, who scattered into flight
The Stars before him from the Field of Night,
  Drives Night along with them from Heav'n and strikes
The Sultán's Turret with a Shaft of Light.

Before the phantom of False morning died,
Methought a Voice within the Tavern cried,
  "When all the Temple is prepared within,
Why nods the drowsy Worshiper outside?"

And, as the Cock crew, those who stood before
The Tavern shouted—"Open, then, the Door!
You know how little while we have to stay,
And, once departed, may return no more."

Come, fill the Cup, and in the fire of Spring
Your Winter garment of Repentance fling;
  The Bird of Time has but a little way
To flutter—and the Bird is on the Wing.

A Book of Verses underneath the Bough,
A Jug of Wine, a Loaf of Bread—and Thou
  Beside me singing in the Wilderness—
O, Wilderness were Paradise enow!

Some for the Glories of This World; and some
Sigh for the Prophet's Paradise to come;
  Ah, take the Cash, and let the Credit go,
Nor heed the rumble of a distant Drum!

Ah, make the most of what we yet may spend,
Before we too into the Dust descend;
  Dust into Dust, and under Dust, to lie,
Sans Wine, sans Song, sans Singer, and—sans End!

Alike for those who for Today prepare,
And those that after some Tomorrow stare,
  A Muezzin from the Tower of Darkness cries,
"Fools, your Reward is neither Here nor There."

Why, all the Saints and Sages who discussed
Of the Two Worlds so wisely—they are thrust
   Like foolish Prophets forth; their Words to Scorn
Are scattered, and their Mouths are stopped with Dust.

Myself when young did eagerly frequent
Doctor and Saint, and heard great argument
   About it and about; but evermore
Came out by the same door where in I went.

With them the seed of Wisdom did I sow,
And with mine own hand wrought to make it grow;
   And this was all the Harvest that I reaped—
"I came like Water, and like Wind I go."

                    —Edward Fitzgerald

In Flanders Fields

In Flanders Fields the poppies blow
Between the crosses, row on row,
   That mark our place; and in the sky
   The larks, still bravely singing, fly
Scarce heard amid the guns below.

We are the Dead. Short days ago
We lived, felt dawn, saw sunset glow,
   Loved and were loved, and now we lie
   In Flanders Fields.

Take up our quarrel with the foe.
To you from failing hands we throw
   The torch; be yours to hold it high.
   If ye break faith with us who die,
We shall not sleep, though poppies grow
   In Flanders Fields.

                    —John McCrae

The Highwayman

PART ONE

The wind was a torrent of darkness among the gusty trees,
The moon was a ghostly galleon tossed upon cloudy seas,
The road was a ribbon of moonlight over the purple moor,
And the highwayman came riding—
> Riding—riding—
The highwayman came riding, up to the old inn door.

He'd a French cocked hat on his forehead, a bunch of lace
  at his chin,
A coat of the claret velvet, and breeches of brown doeskin;
They fitted with never a wrinkle: his boots were up to the
  thigh!
And he rode with a jeweled twinkle,
> His pistol butts a-twinkle,
His rapier hilt a-twinkle, under the jeweled sky.

Over the cobbles he clattered and clashed in the dark inn-
  yard,
And he tapped with his whip on the shutters, but all was
  locked and barred;
He whistled a tune to the window, and who should be
  waiting there
But the landlord's black-eyed daughter,
> Bess, the landlord's daughter,
Plaiting a dark red love knot into her long black hair.

And dark in the dark old innyard a stable wicket creaked
Where Tim, the ostler, listened; his face was white and
  peaked;
His eyes were hollows of madness, his hair like moldy hay,
But he loved the landlord's daughter,
> The landlord's red-lipped daughter;
Dumb as a dog he listened, and he heard the robber say—

"One kiss, my bonny sweetheart, I'm after a prize tonight,
But I shall be back with the yellow gold before the morn-
  ing light;
Yet, if they press me sharply, and harry me through the
  day,

Then look for me by moonlight,
   Watch for me by moonlight,
I'll come to thee by moonlight, though hell should bar the
  way."

He rose upright in the stirrups; he scarce could reach her
  hand,
But she loosened her hair i' the casement! His face burnt
  like a brand
As the black cascade of perfume came tumbling over his
  breast;
And he kissed its waves in the moonlight,
   (Oh, sweet black waves in the moonlight!)
Then he tugged at his reins in the moonlight, and galloped
  away to the West.

PART TWO

He did not come in the dawning; he did not come at noon;
And out o' the tawny sunset, before the rise o' the moon,
When the road was a gipsy's ribbon, looping the purple
  moor,
A redcoat troop came marching—
   Marching—marching—
King George's men came marching, up to the old inn door.

They said no word to the landlord, they drank his ale in-
  stead,
But they gagged his daughter and bound her to the foot of
  her narrow bed;
Two of them knelt at her casement, with muskets at their
  side!
There was death at every window;
   And hell at one dark window;
For Bess could see, through her casement, the road that *he*
  would ride.

They had tied her up to attention, with many a sniggering
  jest;
They had bound a musket beside her, with the muzzle
  beneath her breast!
"Now keep good watch!" and they kissed her. She heard
  the dead man say—
Look for me by moonlight;
   Watch for me by moonlight;

*I'll come to thee by moonlight, though hell should bar the
    way!*

She twisted her hands behind her; but all the knots held
    good!
She writhed her hands till her fingers were wet with sweat
    or blood!
They stretched and strained in the darkness, and the hours
    crawled by like years,
Till, now, on the stroke of midnight,
        Cold on the stroke of midnight,
The tip of one finger touched it! The trigger at least was
    hers!
The tip of one finger touched it; she strove no more for the
    rest!
Up, she stood up to attention, with the muzzle beneath
    her breast,
She would not risk their hearing; she would not strive
    again;
For the road lay bare in the moonlight;
        Blank and bare in the moonlight;
And the blood of her veins in the moonlight throbbed to
    her love's refrain.

Tlot-tlot, tlot-tlot! Had they heard it? The horse-hoofs
    ringing clear;
Tlot-tlot, tlot-tlot, in the distance? Were they deaf that
    they did not hear?
Down the ribbon of moonlight, over the brow of the hill,
The highwayman came riding
        Riding, riding!
The redcoats looked to their priming! She stood up straight
    and still!
Tlot-tlot, in the frosty silence! *Tlot-tlot* in the echoing
    night!
Nearer he came and nearer! Her face was like a light!
Her eyes grew wide for a moment; she drew one last deep
    breath,
Then her finger moved in the moonlight,
        Her musket shattered the moonlight,
Shattered her breast in the moonlight and warned him—
    with her death.
He turned; he spurred him Westward; he did not know
    who stood

Bowed, with her head o'er the musket, drenched with her
   own red blood!
Not till the dawn he heard it, his face grew gray to hear
How Bess, the landlord's daughter,
            The landlord's black-eyed daughter,
Had watched for her love in the moonlight, and died in the
   darkness there.
Back, he spurred like a madman, shrieking a curse to the
   sky,
With the white road smoking behind him, and his rapier
   brandished high!
Blood-red were his spurs in the golden noon; wine-red was
   his velvet coat,
When they shot him down on the highway,
            Down like a dog on the highway,
And he lay in his blood on the highway, with a bunch of
   lace at his throat.

And still of a winter's night, they say, when the wind is in
   the trees,
When the moon is a ghostly galleon tossed upon cloudy
   seas,
When the road is a ribbon of moonlight over the purple
   moor,
A highwayman comes riding—
            Riding—riding—
A highwayman comes riding up to the old inn door.

Over the cobbles he clatters and clangs in the dark innyard;
He taps with his whip on the shutters, but all is locked and
   barred;
He whistles a tune to the window, and who should be
   waiting there
But the landlord's black-eyed daughter,
            Bess, the landlord's daughter,
Plaiting a dark red love knot into her long black hair.
                                        —ALFRED NOYES

79

The Eagle

He clasps the crag with crooked hands;
Close to the sun in lonely lands,
Ringed with the azure world, he stands.

The wrinkled sea beneath him crawls;
He watches from his mountain walls,
And like a thunderbolt he falls.

—ALFRED LORD TENNYSON

Requiem

Under the wide and starry sky,
Dig the grave and let me lie.
Glad did I live and gladly die,
    And I laid me down with a will.

This be the verse you grave for me:
Here he lies where he longed to be,
Home is the sailor, home from sea,
    And the hunter home from the hill.

—ROBERT LOUIS STEVENSON

The Charge of the Light Brigade

Half a league, half a league,
Half a league onward,
All in the valley of Death
    Rode the six hundred.
    "Forward, the Light Brigade!
Charge for the guns!" he said.
Into the valley of Death
    Rode the six hundred.

71

"Forward, the Light Brigade!"
Was there a man dismayed?
Not though the soldier knew
    Someone had blundered.
Theirs not to make reply,
Theirs not to reason why,
Theirs but to do and die.
Into the valley of Death
    Rode the six hundred.

Cannon to right of them,
Cannon to left of them,
Cannon in front of them
    Volleyed and thundered;
Stormed at with shot and shell,
Boldly they rode and well,
Into the jaws of Death,
Into the mouth of Hell
    Rode the six hundred.

Flashed all their sabers bare,
Flashed as they turned in air
Sabring the gunners there,
Charging an army, while
    All the world wondered:
Plunged in the battery smoke
Right through the line they broke;
Cossack and Russian
Reeled from the saber stroke
    Shattered and sundered.
Then they rode back, but not,
    Not the six hundred.

Cannon to right of them,
Cannon to left of them,
Cannon behind them
    Volleyed and thundered;
Stormed at with shot and shell,
While horse and hero fell,
They that had fought so well
Came through the jaws of Death,
Back from the mouth of Hell,
All that was left of them,
    Left of six hundred.

When can their glory fade?
O the wild charge they made!
    All the world wondered.
Honor the charge they made!
Honor the Light Brigade,
    Noble six hundred!

—ALFRED LORD TENNYSON

The Twins

In form and feature, face and limb,
    I grew so like my brother,
That folks got taking me for him,
    And each for one another.
It puzzled all our kith and kin,
    It reached a fearful pitch;
For one of us was born a twin,
    Yet not a soul knew which.

One day, to make the matter worse,
    Before our names were fixed,
As we were being washed by nurse,
    We got completely mixed;
And thus, you see, by fate's decree,
    Or rather nurse's whim,
My brother John got christened me,
    And I got christened him.

This fatal likeness even dogged
    My footsteps when at school,
And I was always getting flogged,
    For John turned out a fool.
I put this question, fruitlessly,
    To everyone I knew,
"What *would* you do, if you were me,
    To prove that you were *you*?"

Our close resemblance turned the tide
    Of my domestic life,
For somehow, my intended bride
    Became my brother's wife.

In fact, year after year the same
   Absurd mistakes went on,
And when I died, the neighbors came
   And buried brother John.
            —HENRY SAMBROOKE LEIGH

Stopping By Woods on a Snowy Evening

Whose woods these are I think I know.
His house is in the village though;
He will not see me stopping here
To watch his woods fill up with snow.

My little horse must think it queer
To stop without a farmhouse near
Between the woods and frozen lake
The darkest evening of the year.

He gives his harness bells a shake
To ask if there is some mistake.
The only other sound's the sweep
Of easy wind and downy flake.

The woods are lovely, dark and deep,
But I have promises to keep,
And miles to go before I sleep,
And miles to go before I sleep.
            —ROBERT FROST

Silver

Slowly, silently, now the moon
Walks the night in her silver shoon;
This way, and that, she peers, and sees
Silver fruit upon silver trees;
One by one the casements catch
Her beams beneath the silvery thatch;
Couched in his kennel, like a log,
With paws of silver sleeps the dog;

From their shadowy cote the white breasts peep
Of doves in a silver-feathered sleep;
A harvest mouse goes scampering by,
With silver claws and a silver eye;
And moveless fish in the water gleam,
By silver reeds in a silver stream.

—WALTER DE LA MARE

The Gray Squirrel

Like a small gray
coffeepot,
sits the squirrel.
He is not

all he should be,
kills by dozens
trees, and eats
his red-brown cousins.

The keeper, on the
other hand
, who shot him, is
a Christian, and

loves his enemies,
which shows
the squirrel was not
one of those.

—HUMBERT WOLFE

Mother to Son

Well, son, I'll tell you:
Life for me ain't been no crystal stair,
It's had tacks in it,
And splinters,
And boards torn up,

And places with no carpets on the floor—
Bare.
But all the time
I'se been a-climbin' on
And reachin' landin's
And turnin' corners,
And sometimes goin' in the dark
Where there ain't been no light.
So, boy, don't you turn back.
Don't you set down on the steps
'Cause you find it kinder hard.
Don't you fall now—
For I'se still goin', honey,
I'se still climbin',
And life for me ain't been no crystal stair.

—LANGSTON HUGHES

By Her Aunt's Grave

"Sixpence a week," says the girl to her lover,
"Aunt used to bring me, for she could confide
In me alone, she vowed. It was to cover
The cost of her headstone when she died.
And that was a year ago last June;
I've not yet fixed it. But I must soon."

"And where is the money now, my dear?"
"O, snug in my purse. . . . Aunt was so slow
In saving it—eighty weeks, or near." . . .
"Let's spend it," he hints. "For she won't know.
There's a dance tonight at the *Load of Hay*."
She passively nods. And they go that way.

—THOMAS HARDY

Meeting at Night

The gray sea and the long black land;
And the yellow half-moon large and low;
And the startled little waves that leap

76

In fiery ringlets from their sleep,
As I gain the cove with pushing prow,
And quench its speed i' the slushy sand.

Then a mile of warm sea-scented beach;
Three fields to cross till a farm appears;
A tap at the pane, the quick sharp scratch
And blue spurt of a lighted match,
And a voice less loud, through its joys and fears,
Than the two hearts beating each to each!

—ROBERT BROWNING

The Lads in Their Hundreds

The lads in their hundreds to Ludlow come in for the fair,
    There's men from the barn and the forge and the mill
        and the fold,
The lads for the girls and the lads for the liquor are there,
    And there with the rest are the lads that will never be
        old.

There's chaps from the town and the field and the till and
        the cart,
    And many to count are the stalwart, and many the
        brave,
And many the handsome of face and the handsome of
        heart,
    And few that will carry their looks or their truth to the
        grave.

I wish one could know them, I wish there were tokens to
        tell
    The fortunate fellows that now you can never discern;
And then one could talk with them friendly and wish them
        farewell
    And watch them depart on the way that they will not re-
        turn.

But now you may stare as you like and there's nothing to
        scan;
    And brushing your elbow unguessed-at and not to be
        told

They carry back bright to the coiner the mintage of man,
The lads that will die in their glory and never be old.

—A. E. HOUSMAN

A Day

I'll tell you how the sun rose,—
A ribbon at a time.
The steeples swam in amethyst,
The news like squirrels ran.

The hills untied their bonnets,
The bobolinks begun.
Then I said softly to myself,
"That must have been the sun!"

. . .

But how he set, I know not.
There seemed a purple stile
Which little yellow boys and girls
Were climbing all the while

Till when they reached the other side,
A dominie in gray
Put gently up the evening bars,
And led the flock away.

—EMILY DICKINSON

Richard Cory

Whenever Richard Cory went downtown,
  We people on the pavement looked at him;
He was a gentleman from sole to crown,
  Clean favored, and imperially slim.

And he was always quietly arrayed,
  And he was always human when he talked;
But still he fluttered pulses when he said,
  "Good morning," and he glittered when he walked.

And he was rich—yes, richer than a king—
  And admirably schooled in every grace:
In fine, we thought that he was everything
  To make us wish that we were in his place.

So on we worked, and waited for the light,
  And went without the meat, and cursed the bread;
And Richard Cory, one calm summer night,
  Went home and put a bullet through his head.

—EDWIN ARLINGTON ROBINSON

The Cremation of Sam McGee

There are strange things done in the midnight sun
  By the men who moil for gold;
The Arctic trails have their secret tales
  That would make your blood run cold;
The Northern Lights have seen queer sights,
  But the queerest they ever did see
Was that night on the marge of Lake Lebarge
  I cremated Sam McGee.

Now Sam McGee was from Tennessee, where the cotton
    blooms and blows.
Why he left his home in the South to roam 'round the
    Pole, God only knows.
He was always cold, but the land of gold seemed to hold
    him like a spell;
Though he'd often say in his homely way that he'd "sooner
    live in hell."

On a Christmas Day we were mushing our way over the
    Dawson trail.
Talk of your cold! through the parka's fold it stabbed like
    a driven nail.
If our eyes we'd close, then the lashes froze till sometimes
    we couldn't see;
It wasn't much fun, but the only one to whimper was Sam
    McGee.

79

And that very night, as we lay packed tight in our robes
    beneath the snow,
And the dogs were fed, and the stars o'erhead were dancing
    heel and toe,
He turned to me, and "Cap," says he, "I'll cash in this
    trip, I guess;
And if I do, I'm asking that you won't refuse my last re-
    quest."

Well, he seemed so low that I couldn't say no; then he
    says with a sort of moan:
"It's the cursèd cold, and it's got right hold till I'm chilled
    clean through to the bone.
Yet 'tain't being dead—it's my awful dread of the icy grave
    that pains;
So I want you to swear that, foul or fair, you'll cremate my
    last remains."

A pal's last need is a thing to heed, so I swore I would not
    fail;
And we started on at the streak of dawn; but God! he
    looked ghastly pale.
He crouched on the sleigh, and he raved all day of his
    home in Tennessee;
And before nightfall a corpse was all that was left of Sam
    McGee.

There wasn't a breath in that land of death, and I hur-
    ried, horror-driven,
With a corpse half hid that I couldn't get rid, because of
    a promise given;
It was lashed to the sleigh, and it seemed to say: "You
    may tax your brawn and brains,
But you promised true, and it's up to you to cremate these
    last remains."

Now a promise made is a debt unpaid, and the trail has its
    own stern code.
In the days to come, though my lips were dumb, in my
    heart how I cursed that load.
In the long, long night, by the lone firelight, while the
    huskies, round in a ring,
Howled out their woes to the homeless snows—O God!
    how I loathed the thing.

And every day that quiet clay seemed to heavy and heavier
grow;
And on I went, though the dogs were spent and the grub
was getting low;
The trail was bad, and I felt half mad, but I swore I would
not give in;
And I'd often sing to the hateful thing, and it hearkened
with a grin.

Till I came to the marge of Lake Lebarge, and a derelict
there lay;
It was jammed in the ice, but I saw in a trice it was called
the "Alice May."
And I looked at it, and I thought a bit, and I looked at my
frozen chum;
Then "Here," said I, with a sudden cry, "is my cre-ma-
tor-eum."

Some planks I tore from the cabin floor, and I lit the boiler
fire;
Some coal I found that was lying around, and I heaped the
fuel higher;
The flames just soared, and the furnace roared—such a
blaze you seldom see;
And I burrowed a hole in the glowing coal, and I stuffed
in Sam McGee.

Then I made a hike, for I didn't like to hear him sizzle so;
And the heavens scowled, and the huskies howled, and the
wind began to blow.
It was icy cold, but the hot sweat rolled down my cheeks,
and I don't know why;
And the greasy smoke in an inky cloak went streaking
down the sky.

I do not know how long in the snow I wrestled with grisly
fear;
But the stars came out and they danced about ere again I
ventured near;
I was sick with dread, but I bravely said: "I'll just take a
peep inside.
I guess he's cooked, and it's time I looked"; . . . then
the door I opened wide.

81

And there sat Sam, looking cool and calm, in the heart of
    the furnace roar;
And he wore a smile you could see a mile, and he said.
    "Please close that door.
It's fine in here, but I greatly fear you'll let in the cold and
    storm—
Since I left Plumtree, down in Tennessee, it's the first time
    I've been warm."

There are strange things done in the midnight sun
    By the men who moil for gold;
The Arctic trails have their secret tales
    That would make your blood run cold;
The Northern Lights have seen queer sights,
    But the queerest they ever did see
Was that night on the marge of Lake Lebarge
    I cremated Sam McGee.

—ROBERT W. SERVICE

Crossing

STOP   LOOK   LISTEN
as gate stripes swing down,
count the cars hauling distance
upgrade through town:
warning whistle, bellclang,
engine eating steam,
engineer waving,
a fast-freight dream:
B&M boxcar,
boxcar again,
Frisco gondola,
eight-nine-ten,
Erie and Wabash,
Seaboard, U.P.,
Pennsy tankcar,
twenty-two, three,
Phoebe Snow, B&O,
thirty-four, five,
Santa Fe cattle

shipped alive,
red cars, yellow cars,
orange cars, black,
Youngstown steel
down to Mobile
on Rock Island track,
fifty-nine, sixty,
hoppers of coke,
Anaconda copper,
hotbox smoke,
eighty-eight,
red-ball freight,
Rio Grande,
Nickel Plate,
Hiawatha,
Lackawanna,
rolling fast
and loose,
ninety-seven,
coal car,
boxcar,
CABOOSE!

—PHILIP BOOTH

Opportunity

This I beheld, or dreamed it in a dream:—
There spread a cloud of dust along a plain;
And underneath the cloud, or in it, raged
A furious battle, and men yelled, and swords
Shocked upon swords and shields. A prince's banner
Wavered, then staggered backward, hemmed by foes.
A craven hung along the battle's edge,
And thought, "Had I a sword of keener steel—
That blue blade that the king's son bears—but this
Blunt thing!" he snapped and flung it from his hand,
And lowering crept away and left the field.
Then came the king's son, wounded, sore bestead,
And weaponless, and saw the broken sword,
Hilt-buried in the dry and trodden sand,
And ran and snatched it, and with battle-shout

83

Lifted afresh he hewed his enemy down,
And saved a great cause that heroic day.
                                    —EDWARD ROWLAND SILL

Danny Deever

"What are the bugles blowin' for?" said Files-on-Parade.
"To turn you out, to turn you out," the Color-Sergeant said.
"What makes you look so white, so white?" said Files-on-Parade.
"I'm dreadin' what I've got to watch," the Color-Sergeant said.

> For they're hangin' Danny Deever, you can 'ear the Dead March play,
> The regiment's in 'ollow square—they're hangin' him today;
> They've taken of his buttons off an' cut his stripes away,
> An' they're hangin' Danny Deever in the mornin'.

"What makes the rear-rank breathe so 'ard!" said Files-on-Parade.
"It's bitter cold, it's bitter cold," the Color-Sergeant said.
"What makes that front-rank man fall down?" says Files-on-Parade.
"A touch of sun, a touch of sun," the Color-Sergeant said.

> They are hangin' Danny Deever, they are marchin' of 'im round.
> They' ave 'alted Danny Deever by 'is coffin on the ground:
> An' 'e'll swing in 'arf a minute for a sneakin' shootin' hound—
> O they're hangin' Danny Deever in the mornin'!

" 'Is cot was right-'and cot to mine," said Files-on-Parade.
" 'E's sleepin' out an' far tonight," the Color-Sergeant said.
"I've drunk 'is beer a score o' times," said Files-on-Parade.
" 'E's drinkin' bitter beer alone," the Color-Sergeant said.

> They are hangin' Danny Deever, you must mark 'im to 'is place,
> For 'e shot a comrade sleepin'—you must look 'im in the face;

Nine 'undred of 'is county an' the regiment's dis-
      grace,
While they're hangin' Danny Deever in the
      mornin'.
"What's that so black agin the sun?" said Files-on-Parade.
"It's Danny fightin' 'ard for life," the Color-Sergeant said.
"What's that that whimpers over'ead?" said File-on-Parade.
"It's Danny's soul that's passin' now," the Color-Sergeant
      said.
    For they're done with Danny Deever, you can
      'ear the quickstep play,
    The regiment's in column, an' they're marchin'
      us away;
    Ho! the young recruits are shakin', an' they'll
      want their beer today,
After hangin' Danny Deever in the mornin'.
                   —RUDYARD KIPLING

Sea-Fever

I must go down to the seas again, to the lonely sea and the
      sky,
And all I ask is a tall ship and a star to steer her by,
And the wheel's kick and the wind's song and the white
      sail's shaking,
And a gray mist on the sea's face and a gray dawn breaking.

I must go down to the seas again, for the call of the run-
      ning tide
Is a wild call and a clear call that may not be denied;
And all I ask is a windy day with the white clouds flying,
And the flung spray and the blown spume, and the seagulls
      crying.

I must go down to the seas again to the vagrant gypsy life,
To the gull's way and the whale's way where the wind's
      like a whetted knife;
And all I ask is a merry yarn from a laughing fellow rover,
And quiet sleep and a sweet dream when the long trick's
      over.

                   —JOHN MASEFIELD

Aprilmonth

April, silly April, giddy and laughing,
skipped down the gardenpath, tripped,
fell, full-face, and scattered all around
white blossom, green leaf, and yellow bud;
picked herself up, the back of one hand
smudging a tear; frowned at my in-
solence, whimpered, and ran away.

—HERBERT BITTERMAN

Casey Jones

Come, all you rounders, if you want to hear
A story 'bout a brave engineer.
Casey Jones was the rounder's name
On a six-eight wheeler, boys, he won his fame.
The caller called Casey at a half past four,
Kissed his wife at the station door,
Mounted to the cabin with his orders in his hand,
And he took his farewell trip to that promised land:

CHORUS:

Casey Jones, mounted to the cabin,
Casey Jones, with his orders in his hand,
Casey Jones, mounted to the cabin,
And he took his farewell trip to the promised land.

"Put in your water and shovel in your coal,
Put your head out the window, watch them drivers roll,
I'll run her till she leaves the rail
'Cause I'm eight hours late with that western mail."
He looked at his watch and his watch was slow,
He looked at the water and the water was low,
He turned to the fireman and then he said,
"We're goin' to reach Frisco but we'll all be dead":

CHORUS:

Casey Jones, goin' to reach Frisco,
Casey Jones, but we'll all be dead,

Casey Jones, goin' to reach Frisco,
"We're goin' to reach Frisco, but we'll all be dead."

Casey pulled up that Reno Hill,
He tooted for the crossing with an awful shrill,
The switchman knew by the engine's moan
That the man at the throttle was Casey Jones.
He pulled up within two miles of the place
Number Four stared him right in the face,
He turned to the fireman, said, "Boy, you better jump,
'Cause there's two locomotives that's a-goin' to bump":

CHORUS:

Casey Jones, two locomotives,
Casey Jones, that's a-goin' to bump,
Casey Jones, two locomotives,
"There's two locomotives that's a-goin' to bump."

Casey said just before he died,
"There's two more roads that I'd like to ride."
The fireman said, "What could they be?"
"The Southern Pacific and the Sante Fe."
Mrs. Casey sat on her bed a-sighin',
Just received a message that Casey was dyin'.
Said, "Go to bed, children, and hush your cry'n,
'Cause you got another papa on the Salt Lake Line":

CHORUS:

Mrs. Casey Jones, got another papa,
Mrs. Casey Jones, on that Salt Lake Line,
Mrs. Casey Jones, got another papa,
"And you've got another papa on the Salt Lake Line."

—ANONYMOUS

When I Heard the Learn'd Astronomer

When I heard the learn'd astronomer,
When the proofs, the figures, were ranged in columns
    before me,
When I was shown the charts and diagrams, to add, divide,
    and measure them,

When I sitting heard the astronomer where he lectured
   with much applause in the lecture room,

How soon unaccountable I became tired and sick,
Till rising and gliding out I wander'd off by myself,
In the mystical moist night air, and from time to time,
Look'd up in perfect silence at the stars.

—WALT WHITMAN

When the Frost Is on the Punkin

When the frost is on the punkin and the fodder's in the
   shock,
And you hear the kyouck and the gobble of the struttin'
   turkey cock
And the clackin' of the guineys, and the cluckin' of the
   hens,
And the rooster's hallylooyer as he tiptoes on the fence;
O, it's then's the times a feller is a-feelin' at his best,
With the risin' sun to greet him from a night of peaceful
   rest,
As he leaves the house, bareheaded, and goes out to feed
   the stock,
When the frost is on the punkin and the fodder's in the
   shock!

They's something kindo' harty-like about the atmusfere
When the heat of summer's over and the coolin' fall is
   here—
Of course we miss the flowers, and the blossums on the
   trees,
And the mumble of the hummin'birds and the buzzin' of
   the bees;
But the air's so appetizin'; and the landscape through the
   haze
Of a crisp and sunny mornin' of the airly autumn days
Is a pictur' that no painter has the colorin' to mock—
When the frost is on the punkin and the fodder's in the
   shock!

The husky, rusty russel of the tossels of the corn,
And the raspin' of the tangled leaves, as golden as the
    morn;
The stubble in the furries—kindo' lonesome-like, but still
A-preachin' sermons to us of the barns they growed to fill;
The strawstacks in the medder, and the reaper in the shed;
The hosses in theyr stalls below—the clover overhead!—
O, it sets my hart a-clickin' like the tickin' of a clock,
When the frost is on the punkin and the fodder's in the
    shock!

Then your apples all is gethered, and the ones a feller
    keeps
Is poured around the celler-floor in red and yeller heaps;
And your cider-makin's over, and your wimmern-folks is
    through
With their mince and applebutter, and theyr souse and
    saussage, too! . . .
I don't know how to tell it—but ef sich a thing could be
As the Angels wantin' boardin', and they'd call around on
    me—
I'd want to 'commodate 'em—all the whole-indurin'
    flock—
When the frost is on the punkin and the fodder's in the
    shock!

—James Whitcomb Riley

Stupidity Street

I saw with open eyes
Singing birds sweet
Sold in the shops
For the people to eat,
Sold in the shops of
Stupidity Street.

I saw in a vision
The worm in the wheat,
And in the shops nothing
For people to eat:
Nothing for sale in
Stupidity Street.

—Ralph Hodgson

The Ballad of East and West

Oh, East is East, and West is West, and never the twain
    shall meet,
Till Earth and Sky stand presently at God's great Judg-
    ment Seat;
But there is neither East nor West, Border, nor Breed,
    nor Birth,
When two strong men stand face to face, though they
    come from the ends of the earth!

Kamal is out with twenty men to raise the Border side,
And he has lifted the Colonel's mare that is the Colonel's
    pride.
He has lifted her out of the stable door between the dawn
    and the day,
And turned the calkins upon her feet, and ridden her far
    away.
Then up spoke the Colonel's son that led a troop of the
    Guides:
"Is there never a man of all my men can say where
    Kamal hides?"
Then up and spoke Mohammed Khan, the son of the
    Ressaldar,
"If ye know the track of the morning mist, ye know where
    his pickets are.
At dusk he harries the Abazai—at dawn he is into Bonair,
But he must go by Fort Bukloh to his own place to fare,
So if ye gallop to Fort Bukloh as fast as a bird can fly,
By the favor of God ye may cut him off ere he win to
    the Tongue of Jagai.
But if he be passed the Tongue of Jagai, right swiftly turn
    ye then,
For the length and the breadth of that grisly plain is
    sown with Kamal's men.
There is rock to the left, and rock to the right, and low
    lean thorn between,
And ye may hear a breech bolt snick where never a man
    is seen."
The Colonel's son has taken horse, and a raw rough dun
    was he,
With the mouth of a bell and the heart of Hell, and the
    head of the gallows tree.

The Colonel's son to the Fort has won, they bid him
    stay to eat—
Who rides at the tail of a Border thief, he sits not long
    at his meat.
He's up and away from Fort Bukloh as fast as he can fly,
Till he was aware of his father's mare in the gut of the
    Tongue of Jagai,
Till he was aware of his father's mare with Kamal upon
    her back,
And when he could spy the white of her eye, he made
    the pistol crack.
He has fired once, he has fired twice, but the whistling
    ball went wide.
"Ye shoot like a soldier," Kamal said. "Show now if ye
    can ride!"
It's up and over the Tongue of Jagai, as blown dust-
    devils go,
The dun he fled like a stag of ten, but the mare like a
    barren doe.
The dun he leaned against the bit and slugged his head
    above,
But the red mare played with the snaffle bars, as a maiden
    plays with a glove.
There was rock to the left and rock to the right, and low
    lean thorn between,
And thrice he heard a breech bolt snick tho' never a man
    was seen.
They have ridden the low moon out of the sky, their hoofs
    drum up the dawn,
The dun he went like a wounded bull, but the mare like
    a new-roused fawn.
The dun he fell at a watercourse—in a woeful heap fell he,
And Kamal has turned the red mare back, and pulled the
    rider free.
He has knocked the pistol out of his hand—small room
    was there to strive,
" 'Twas only by favor of mine," quoth he, "ye rode so long
    alive:
There was not a rock for twenty mile, there was not a
    clump of tree,
But covered a man of my own men with his rifle cocked
    on his knee.
If I had raised my bridle hand, as I have held it low,
The little jackals that flee so fast were feasting all in a row.

If I had bowed my head on my breast, as I have held it
  high,
The kite that whistles above us now were gorged till she
  could not fly."
Lightly answered the Colonel's son: "Do good to bird and
  beast,
But count who come for the broken meats before thou
  makest a feast.
If there should follow a thousand swords to carry my bones
  away,
Belike the price of a jackal's meal were more than a thief
  could pay.
They will feed their horse on the standing crop, their
  men on the garnered grain,
The thatch of the byres will serve their fires when all the
  cattle are slain.
But if thou thinkest the price be fair,—thy brethren wait
  to sup,
The hound is kin to the jackal spawn,—howl, dog, and
  call them up!
And if thou thinkest the price be high, in steer and gear
  and stack,
Give me my father's mare again, and I'll fight my own
  way back!"
Kamal has gripped him by the hand and set him upon his
  feet.
"No talk shall be of dogs," said he, "when wolf and gray
  wolf meet.
May I eat dirt if thou hast hurt of me in deed or breath;
What dam of lances brought thee forth to jest at the dawn
  with Death?"
Lightly answered the Colonel's son: "I hold by the blood
  of my clan:
Take up the mare for my father's gift—by God, she
  has carried a man!"
The red mare ran to the Colonel's son, and nuzzled against
  his breast;
"We be two strong men," said Kamal then, "but she
  loveth the younger best.
So she shall go with a lifter's dower, my turquoise-studded
  rein,
My 'broidered saddle and saddlecloth, and silver stirrups
  twain."
The Colonel's son a pistol drew, and held it muzzle end,

"Ye have taken the one from a foe," said he. "Will ye
   take the mate from a friend?"
"A gift for a gift," said Kamal straight; "a limb for the
   risk of a limb.
Thy father has sent his son to me, I'll send my son to
   him!"
With that he whistled his only son, that dropped from a
   mountain crest—
He trod the ling like a buck in spring, and he looked like
   a lance in rest.
"Now here is thy master," Kamal said, "who leads a troop
   of the Guides,
And thou must ride at his left side as shield on shoulder
   rides.
Till Death or I cut loose the tie, at camp and board and
   bed,
Thy life is his—thy fate it is to guard him with thy head.
So, thou must eat the White Queen's meat, and all her
   foes are thine,
And thou must harry thy father's hold for the peace of
   the Border line.
And thou must make a trooper tough and hack thy way
   to power—
Belike they will raise thee to Ressaldar when I am hanged
   in Peshawur!"

They have looked each other between the eyes, and there
   they found no fault.
They have taken the Oath of the Brother-in-Blood on
   leavened bread and salt:
They have taken the Oath of the Brother-in-Blood on
   fire and fresh-cut sod,
On the hilt and the haft of the Khyber knife, and the
   Wondrous Names of God.
The Colonel's son he rides the mare and Kamal's boy the
   dun,
And two have come back to Fort Bukloh where there went
   forth but one.
And when they drew to the Quarter-Guard, full twenty
   swords flew clear—
There was not a man but carried his feud with the blood
   of the mountaineer.
"Ha' done! Ha' done!" said the Colonel's son. "Put up
   the steel at your sides!

Last night ye had struck at a Border thief—tonight 'tis
a man of the Guides!"

Oh, East is East, and West is West, and never the twain
shall meet,
Till Earth and Sky stand presently at God's great Judg-
ment Seat;
But there is neither East nor West, Border, nor Breed,
nor Birth,
When two strong men stand face to face, though they
come from the ends of the earth!

—Rudyard Kipling

After Great Pain a Formal
Feeling Comes

After great pain a formal feeling comes—
The nerves sit ceremonious like tombs;
The stiff heart questions—was it He that bore?
And yesterday—or centuries before?

The feet mechanical go round
A wooden way,
Of ground or air of Ought,
Regardless grown;
A quartz contentment like a stone.

This is the hour of lead
Remembered if outlived
As freezing persons recollect
The snow—
First chill, then stupor, then
The letting go.

—Emily Dickinson

Limited

I am riding on a limited express, one of the crack trains of
    the nation.
Hurtling across the prairie into blue haze and dark air go
    fifteen all-steel coaches holding a thousand people.
(All the coaches shall be scrap and rust and all the men
    and women laughing in the diners and sleepers shall
    pass to ashes.)
I ask a man in the smoker where he is going and he
    answers: "Omaha."

—CARL SANDBURG

The Snow

It sifts from leaden sieves,
It powders all the wood,
It fills with alabaster wool
The wrinkles of the road.

It makes an even face
Of mountain and of plain,—
Unbroken forehead from the east
Unto the east again.

It reaches to the fence,
It wraps it, rail by rail,
Till it is lost in fleeces;
It flings a crystal veil

On stump and stack and stem,—
The summer's empty room,
Acres of seams where harvests were,
Recordless, but for them.
It ruffles wrists of posts,
As ankles of a queen,—
Then stills its artisans like ghosts,
Denying they have been.

—EMILY DICKINSON

95

Homesick Blues

De railroad bridge's
A sad song in de air.
De railroad bridge's
A sad song in de air.
Ever' time de trains pass
I wants to go somewhere.

I went down to de station;
Ma heart was in ma mouth.
Went down to de station;
Heart was in ma mouth.
Lookin' for a box car
To roll me to de South.

Homesick blues, Lawd,
'S a terrible thing to have.
Homesick blues is
A terrible thing to have.
To keep from cryin'
I opens ma mouth an' laughs.

—LANGSTON HUGHES

I'm Nobody! Who Are You?

I'm nobody! Who are you?
Are you nobody too?
Then there's a pair of us—don't tell!
They'd banish us, you know.

How dreary to be somebody!
How public, like a frog
To tell your name the livelong day
To an admiring bog!

—EMILY DICKINSON

Mia Carlotta

Giuseppe, da barber, ees greata for "mash,"
He gotta da bigga, da blacka moustache,
Good clo'es an' good styla an' playnta good cash.

W'enevra Giuseppe ees walk on da street,
Da peopla dey talka, "How nobby! how neat!
How softa da handa, how smalla da feet."

He leefta hees hat an' he shaka hees curls,
An' smila weeth teetha so shiny like pearls;
Oh, many da heart of da seely young girls
         He gotta.
      Yes, playnta he gotta—
        But notta
        Carlotta!

Giuseppe, da barber, he maka da eye,
An' like de steam engine puffa an' sigh,
For catcha Carlotta w'en she ees go by.

Carlotta she walka weeth nose in da air,
An' look through Giuseppe weeth faraway stare,
As eef she no see dere ees som'body dere.

Giuseppe, da barber, he gotta da cash,
He gotta da clo'es an' da bigga moustache,
He gotta da seely young girls for da "mash,"
        But notta—
      You bat my life, notta—
        Carlotta.
        I gotta!
        —Thomas Augustine Daly

Smells

Why is it that the poets tell
So little of the sense of smell?
These are the odors I love well:

The smell of coffee freshly ground;
Of rich plum pudding, holly-crowned;
Or onions fried and deeply browned.

The fragrance of a fumy pipe;
The smell of apples, newly ripe;
And printer's ink on leaden type.

Woods by moonlight in September
Breathe most sweet; and I remember
Many a smoky campfire ember.
Camphor, turpentine, and tea,
The balsam of a Christmas tree,
These are whiffs of gramarye . . .
A ship smells best of all to me!

— CHRISTOPHER MORLEY

Barter

Life has loveliness to sell,
All beautiful and splendid things,
Blue waves whitened on a cliff,
Soaring fire that sways and sings,
And children's faces looking up
Holding wonder like a cup.

Life has loveliness to sell,
Music like a curve of gold,
Scent of pine trees in the rain,
Eyes that love you, arms that hold,
And for your spirit's still delight,
Holy thoughts that star the night.

Spend all you have for loveliness,
Buy it and never count the cost;
For one white singing hour of peace
Count many a year of strife well lost,
And for a breath of ecstasy
Give all you have been, or could be.

— SARA TEASDALE

Since There's No Help

Since there's no help, come let us kiss and part.
Nay, I have done, you get no more of me!
And I am glad, yea, glad with all my heart,
That thus so cleanly I myself can free.
Shake hands for ever! Cancel all our vows!
And when we meet at any time again,
Be it not seen in either of our brows
That we one jot of former love retain.
Now at the last gasp of Love's latest breath,
When, his pulse failing, Passion speechless lies,
When Faith is kneeling by his bed of death,
And Innocence is closing up his eyes—
    Now, if thou would'st, when all have given him over,
    From death to life thou might'st him yet recover!

—MICHAEL DRAYTON

Night Song at Amalfi

I asked the heaven of stars
    What I should give my love—
It answered me with silence,
    Silence above.

I asked the darkened sea
    Down where the fishermen go—
It answered me with silence,
    Silence below.

Oh, I could give him weeping,
    Or I could give him song—
But how can I give silence
    My whole life long?

—SARA TEASDALE

The Man with the Hoe

(WRITTEN AFTER SEEING MILLET'S
WORLD-FAMOUS PAINTING)

Bowed by the weight of centuries he leans
Upon his hoe and gazes on the ground,
The emptiness of ages in his face,
And on his back the burden of the world.
Who made him dead to rapture and despair,
A thing that grieves not and that never hopes,
Stolid and stunned, a brother to the ox?
Who loosened and let down this brutal jaw?
Whose was the hand that slanted back this brow?
Whose breath blew out the light within this brain?

Is this the Thing the Lord God made and gave
To have dominion over sea and land;
To trace the stars and search the heavens for power;
To feel the passion of Eternity?
Is this the dream He dreamed who shaped the suns
And marked their ways upon the ancient deep?
Down all the caverns of Hell to their last gulf
There is no shape more terrible than this—
More tongued with censure of the world's blind greed—
More filled with signs and portents for the soul—
More packt with danger to the universe.

What gulfs between him and the seraphim!
Slave of the wheel of labor, what to him
Are Plato and the swing of Pleiades?
What the long reaches of the peaks of song,
The rift of dawn, the reddening of the rose?
Through this dread shape the suffering ages look;
Time's tragedy is in that aching stoop;
Through this dread shape humanity betrayed,
Plundered, profaned, and disinherited,
Cries protest to the Judges of the World,
A protest that is also prophecy.

O masters, lords, and rulers in all lands,
Is this the handiwork you give to God,
This monstrous thing distorted and soul-quenched?

How will you ever straighten up this shape;
Touch it again with immortality;
Give back the upward looking and the light;
Rebuild in it the music and the dream;
Make right the immemorial infamies,
Perfidious wrongs, immedicable woes?

O masters, lords, and rulers in all lands,
How will the Future reckon with this man?
How answer his brute question in that hour
When whirlwinds of rebellion shake all shores?
How will it be with kingdoms and with kings—
With those who shaped him to the thing he is—
When this dumb terror shall rise to judge the world,
After the silence of the centuries?

—EDWIN MARKHAM

Jabberwocky

'Twas brillig, and the slithy toves
    Did gyre and gimble in the wabe;
All mimsy were the borogoves,
    And the mome raths outgrabe.

"Beware the Jabberwock, my son!
    The jaws that bite, the claws that catch!
Beware the Jubjub bird, and shun
    The frumious Bandersnatch!"

He took his vorpal sword in hand:
    Long time the manxome foe he sought,—
So rested he by the Tumtum tree,
    And stood awhile in thought.

And as in uffish thought he stood,
    The Jabberwock, with eyes of flame,
Came whiffling through the tulgey wood,
    And burbled as it came!

One, two! One, two! And through and through
    The vorpal blade went snicker-snack!
He left it dead, and with its head
    He went galumphing back.

"And hast thou slain the Jabberwock?
    Come to my arms, my beamish boy!
O frabjous day! Callooh! Callay!"
    He chortled in his joy.

'Twas brillig, and the slithy toves
    Did gyre and gimble in the wabe;
All mimsy were the borogoves,
    And the mome raths outgrabe.

                —LEWIS CARROLL

Oh, When I Was in Love with You

Oh, when I was in love with you,
    Then I was clean and brave,
And miles around the wonder grew
    How well did I behave.

And now the fancy passes by,
    And nothing will remain,
And miles around they'll say that I
    Am quite myself again.

                —A. E. HOUSMAN

The Lord Chancellor's Song

(FROM *Iolanthe*)

When you're lying awake with a dismal headache, and re-
    pose is taboo'd by anxiety,
I conceive you may use any language you choose to indulge
    in without impropriety;

For your brain is on fire—the bedclothes conspire of usual
   slumber to plunder you:
First your counterpane goes, and uncovers your toes, and
   your sheet slips demurely from under you;
Then the blanketing tickles—you feel like mixed pickles—
   so terribly sharp is the pricking,
And you're hot, and you're cross, and you tumble and toss
   till there's nothing 'twixt you and the tickling.
Then the bedclothes all creep to the ground in a heap,
   and you pick 'em all up in a tangle;
Next your pillow resigns and politely declines to remain at
   its usual angle!
Well, you get some repose in the form of a doze, with
   hot eyeballs and head ever aching,
But your slumbering teems with such horrible dreams that
   you'd very much better be waking;
For you dream you are crossing the Channel, and tossing
   about in a steamer from Harwich—
Which is something between a large bathing machine and
   a very small second-class carriage—
And you're giving a treat (penny ice and cold meat) to a
   party of friends and relations—
They're a ravenous horde—and they all came on board at
   Sloane Square and South Kensington Stations.
And bound on that journey you find your attorney (who
   started that morning from Devon);
He's a bit undersized, and you don't feel surprised when
   he tells you he's only eleven.
Well, you're driving like mad with this singular lad (by-
   the-bye the ship's now a four-wheeler),
And you're playing round games, and he calls you bad
   names when you tell him that "ties pay the dealer";
But this you can't stand, so you throw up your hand, and
   you find you're as cold as an icicle,
In your shirt and your socks (the black silk with gold
   clocks), crossing Salisbury Plain on a bicycle:
And he and the crew are on bicycles too—which they have
   somehow or other invested in—
And he's telling the tars all the particulars of a company
   he's interested in—
It's a scheme of devices, to get at low prices, all goods from
   cough mixtures to cables
(Which tickled the sailors) by treating retailers, as though
   they were all vegetables—

You get a good spadesman to plant a small tradesman
    (first take off his boots with a boot-tree),
And his legs will take root, and his fingers will shoot, and
    they'll blossom and bud like a fruit-tree—
From the green-grocer tree you get grapes and greenpea,
    cauliflowers, pineapples, and cranberries,
While the pastrycook plant, cherry brandy will grant, apple
    puffs, and three-corners, and Banberries—
The shares are a penny, and ever so many are taken by
    Rothschild and Baring,
And just as a few are allotted to you, you awake with a
    shudder despairing—
You're a regular wreck, with a crick in your neck, and no
    wonder you snore, for your head's on the floor, and
    you've needles and pins from your soles to your
    shins, and your flesh is a-creep, and your left leg's
    asleep, and you've cramps in your toes, and a fly on
    your nose, and some fluff in your lung, and a fever-
    ish tongue, and a thirst that's intense, and a general
    sense that you haven't been sleeping in clover;
But the darkness has passed, and it's daylight at last, and
    the night has been long—ditto, ditto my song—
    and thank goodness they're both of them over!

—WILLIAM S. GILBERT

POEMS
FOR A SECOND LOOK

Prayer Before Birth

I am not yet born; O hear me.
Let not the bloodsucking bat or the rat or the stoat or the
    clubfooted ghoul come near me.

I am not yet born, console me.
I fear that the human race may with tall walls wall me,
    with strong drugs dope me, with wise lies lure me,
      on black racks rack me, in blood baths roll me.

I am not yet born; provide me
With water to dandle me, grass to grow for me, trees to talk
    to me, sky to sing to me, birds and a white light
      in the back of my mind to guide me.

I am not yet born; forgive me
For the sins that in me the world shall commit, my words
    when they speak me, my thoughts when they think me,
      my treason engendered by traitors beyond me,
        my life when they murder by means of my
        hands, my death when they live me.

I am not yet born; rehearse me
In the parts I must play and the cues I must take when
    old men lecture me, bureaucrats hector me, mountains
      frown at me, lovers laugh at me, the white
        waves call me to folly and the desert calls
        me to doom and the beggar refuses
        my gift and my children curse me.

I am not yet born; O hear me,
Let not the man who is beast or who thinks he is God
    come near me.

I am not yet born; O fill me
With strength against those who would freeze my
    humanity, would dragoon me into a lethal automaton,
      would make me a cog in a machine, a thing with
      one face, a thing, and against all those
        who would dissipate my entirety, would
        blow me like thistledown hither and
        thither or hither and thither
        like water held in the
        hand would spill me.

Let them not make me a stone and let them not spill me.
Otherwise kill me.

—Louis MacNeice

Spring and Fall:

TO A YOUNG CHILD

Márgarét, are you gríeving
Over Goldengrove unleaving?
Leáves, líke the things of man, you
With your fresh thoughts care for, can you?
Áh! ás the heart grows older
It will come to such sights colder
By and by, nor spare a sigh
Though worlds of wanwood leafmeal lie;
And yet you wíll weep and know why.
Now no matter, child, the name:
Sórrow's spríngs áre the same.
Nor mouth had, no nor mind, expressed
What heart heard of, ghost guessed:
It ís the blight man was born for,
It is Margaret you mourn for.

—Gerard Manley Hopkins

The Death of the Ball Turret Gunner

From my mother's sleep I fell into the State,
And I hunched in its belly till my wet fur froze.
Six miles from earth, loosed from its dream of life,
I woke to black flak and the nightmare fighters.
When I died they washed me out of the turret with a hose.

—Randall Jarrell

On First Looking Into Chapman's Homer

Much have I travell'd in the realms of gold,
And many goodly states and kingdoms seen;
Round many western islands have I been
Which bards in fealty to Apollo hold.
Oft of one wide expanse had I been told
That deep-browed Homer ruled as his demesne;
Yet did I never breathe its pure serene
Till I heard Chapman speak out loud and bold:
Then felt I like some watcher of the skies
When a new planet swims into his ken;
Or like stout Cortez when with eagle eyes
He star'd at the Pacific—and all his men
Look'd at each other with a wild surmise—
Silent, upon a peak in Darien.

—John Keats

Ode to a Nightingale

My heart aches, and a drowsy numbness pains
    My sense, as though of hemlock I had drunk,
Or emptied some dull opiate to the drains
    One minute past, and Lethe-wards had sunk:
'Tis not through envy of thy happy lot,
    But being too happy in thine happiness,—
        That thou, light-wingèd Dryad of the trees,
                In some melodious plot
    Of beechen green, and shadows numberless,
        Singest of summer in full-throated ease.

O, for a draught of vintage! that hath been
    Cool'd a long age in the deep-delvèd earth,
Tasting of Flora and the country green,
    Dance, and Provençal song, and sunburnt mirth!
O for a beaker full of the warm South,
    Full of the true, the blushful Hippocrene,
        With beaded bubbles winking at the brim,
                And purple-stainèd mouth;

That I might drink, and leave the world unseen,
  And with thee fade away into the forest dim:

Fade far away, dissolve, and quite forget
  What thou among the leaves hast never known,
The weariness, the fever, and the fret
  Here, where men sit and hear each other groan;
Where palsy shakes a few, sad, last gray hairs,
  Where youth grows pale, and specter-thin, and dies;
    Where but to think is to be full of sorrow
      And leaden-eyed despairs,
  Where Beauty cannot keep her lustrous eyes,
    Or new Love pine at them beyond tomorrow.

Away! away! for I will fly to thee,
  Not charioted by Bacchus and his pards,
But on the viewless wings of Poesy,
  Though the dull brain perplexes and retards:
Already with thee! tender is the night,
  And haply the Queen-Moon is on her throne,
    Cluster'd around by all her starry Fays;
      But here there is no light,
  Save what from heaven is with the breezes blown
    Through verdurous glooms and winding mossy ways.

I cannot see what flowers are at my feet,
  Nor what soft incense hangs upon the boughs,
But, in embalmèd darkness, guess each sweet
  Wherewith the seasonable month endows
The grass, the thicket, and the fruit tree wild;
  White hawthorn, and the pastoral eglantine;
    Fast fading violets cover'd up in leaves;
      And mid-May's eldest child,
  The coming musk rose, full of dewy wine,
    The murmurous haunt of flies on summer eves.

Darkling I listen; and, for many a time
  I have been half in love with easeful Death,
Call'd him soft names in many a musèd rhyme,
  To take into the air my quiet breath;
Now more than ever seems it rich to die,
  To cease upon the midnight with no pain,
    While thou art pouring forth thy soul abroad
      In such an ecstasy!

Still wouldst thou sing, and I have ears in vain—
    To thy high requiem become a sod.

Thou wast not born for death, immortal Bird!
    No hungry generations tread thee down;
The voice I hear this passing night was heard
    In ancient days by emperor and clown:
Perhaps the selfsame song that found a path
    Through the sad heart of Ruth, when, sick for home,
        She stood in tears amid the alien corn;
            The same that ofttimes hath
    Charm'd magic casements, opening on the foam
        Of perilous seas, in faery lands forlorn.

Forlorn! the very word is like a bell
    To toll me back from thee to my sole self!
Adieu! the fancy cannot cheat so well
    As she is fam'd to do, deceiving elf.
Adieu! adieu! thy plaintive anthem fades
    Past the near meadows, over the still stream,
        Up the hillside; and now 'tis buried deep
            In the next valley glades:
    Was it a vision, or a waking dream?
        Fled is that music:—Do I wake or sleep?

—JOHN KEATS

Musée des Beaux Arts

About suffering they were never wrong,
The Old Masters: how well they understood
Its human position; how it takes place
While someone else is eating or opening a window or just
        walking dully along;
How, when the aged are reverently, passionately waiting
For the miraculous birth, there always must be
Children who did not specially want it to happen, skating
On a pond at the edge of the wood:
They never forgot
That even the dreadful martyrdom must run its course
Anyhow in a corner, some untidy spot

111

Where the dogs go on with their doggy life and the tor-
　　turer's horse
Scratches its innocent behind on a tree.

In Brueghel's *Icarus,* for instance: how everything turns
　　away
Quite leisurely from the disaster; the ploughman may
Have heard the splash, the forsaken cry,
But for him it was not an important failure; the sun shone
As it had to on the white legs disappearing into the green
Water; and the expensive delicate ship that must have seen
Something amazing, a boy falling out of the sky,
Had somewhere to get to and sailed calmly on.

　　　　　　　　　　　　　　　—W. H. AUDEN

The Twa Corbies

As I was walking all alane,[1]
I heard twa corbies[2] making a mane;[3]
The tane[4] unto the t'other say,
"Where sall we gang[5] and dine today?"

"In behint yon auld fail dyke,[6]
I wot[7] there lies a new-slain knight;
And naebody kens[8] that he lies there,
But his hawk, his hound, and lady fair.

"His hound is to the hunting gane,
His hawk to fetch the wild-fowl hame,
His lady's ta'en another mate,
So we may mak our dinner sweet.

"Ye'll sit on his white hause-bane,[9]
And I'll pick out his bonny blue een;[10]
Wi ae[11] lock o' his gowden[12] hair
We'll theek[13] our nest when it grows bare.

[1] alone	[6] old turf wall	[10] eyes
[2] two ravens	[7] know	[11] With one
[3] moan	[8] knows	[12] golden
[4] one	[9] neck-bone	[13] thatch
[5] shall we go		

"Mony a one for him makes mane,
But nane sall ken where he is gane;
O'er his white banes when they are bare,
The wind sall blaw for evermair."

—ANONYMOUS

Janet Waking

Beautifully Janet slept
Till it was deeply morning. She woke then
And thought about her dainty-feathered hen,
To see how it had kept.

One kiss she gave her mother,
Only a small one gave she to her daddy
Who would have kissed each curl of his shining baby;
No kiss at all for her brother.

"Old Chucky, Old Chucky!" she cried,
Running on little pink feet upon the grass
To Chucky's house, and listening. But alas,
Her Chucky had died.

It was a transmogrifying bee
Came droning down on Chucky's old bald head
And sat and put the poison. It scarcely bled,
But how exceedingly

And purply did the knot
Swell with the venom and communicate
Its rigor! Now the poor comb stood up straight
But Chucky did not.

So there was Janet
Kneeling on the wet grass, crying her brown hen
(Translated far beyond the daughters of men)
To rise and walk upon it.

And weeping fast as she had breath
Janet implored us, "Wake her from her sleep!"

113

And would not be instructed in how deep
Was the forgetful kingdom of death.

—John Crowe Ransom

Design

I found a dimpled spider, fat and white,
On a white heal-all, holding up a moth
Like a white piece of rigid satin cloth—
Assorted characters of death and blight
Mixed ready to begin the morning right,
Like the ingredients of a witch's broth—
A snow-drop spider, a flower like froth,
And dead wings carried like a paper kite.

What had that flower to do with being white,
The wayside blue and innocent heal-all?
What brought the kindred spider to that height,
Then steered the white moth thither in the night?
What but design of darkness to appall?—
If design govern in a thing so small.

—Robert Frost

Ozymandias

I met a traveler from an antique land
Who said: Two vast and trunkless legs of stone
Stand in the desert. Near them, on the sand,
Half sunk, a shattered visage lies, whose frown,
And wrinkled lip, and sneer of cold command,
Tell that its sculptor well those passions read
Which yet survive, stamped on these lifeless things,
The hand that mocked them and the heart that fed:
And on the pedestal these words appear:
"My name is Ozymandias, king of kings:
Look on my works, ye Mighty, and despair!"

Nothing beside remains. Round the decay
Of that colossal wreck, boundless and bare
The lone and level sands stretch far away.

—PERCY BYSSHE SHELLEY

The Wild Swans at Coole

The trees are in their autumn beauty,
The woodland paths are dry,
Under the October twilight the water
Mirrors a still sky;
Upon the brimming water among the stones
Are nine and fifty swans.

The nineteenth autumn has come upon me
Since I first made my count;
I saw, before I had well finished,
All suddenly mount
And scatter, wheeling, in great broken rings
Upon their clamorous wings.

I have looked upon those brilliant creatures,
And now my heart is sore.
All's changed since I, hearing at twilight,
The first time on this shore,
The bell-beat of their wings above my head,
Trod with a lighter tread.

Unwearied still, lover by lover,
They paddle in the cold,
Companionable streams or climb the air;
Their hearts have not grown old;
Passion or conquest, wander where they will,
Attend upon them still.

But now they drift on the still water
Mysterious, beautiful;
Among what rushes will they build,
By what lake's edge or pool
Delight men's eyes, when I awake some day
To find they have flown away?

—WILLIAM BUTLER YEATS

My Mistress' Eyes Are Nothing Like the Sun

(SONNET 130)

My mistress' eyes are nothing like the sun;
Coral is far more red than her lips' red;
If snow be white, why then her breasts are dun;
If hairs be wires, black wires grow on her head.
I have seen roses damasked, red and white,
But no such roses see I in her cheeks;
And in some perfumes is there more delight
Than in the breath that from my mistress reeks.
I love to hear her speak, yet well I know
That music hath a far more pleasing sound;
I grant I never saw a goddess go;
My mistress, when she walks, treads on the ground.
    And yet, by heaven, I think my love as rare
    As any she belied with false compare.

               —WILLIAM SHAKESPEARE

When to the Sessions of Sweet Silent Thought

(SONNET 30)

When to the sessions of sweet silent thought
I summon up remembrance of things past,
I sigh the lack of many a thing I sought,
And with old woes new wail my dear time's waste:
Then can I drown an eye, unused to flow,
For precious friends hid in death's dateless night,
And weep afresh love's long-since-cancell'd woe,
And moan th' expense of many a vanish'd sight:
Then can I grieve at grievances foregone,
And heavily from woe to woe tell o'er
The sad account of fore-bemoanèd moan,
Which I new pay as if not paid before.
    But if the while I think on thee, dear friend,
    All losses are restored and sorrows end.

               —WILLIAM SHAKESPEARE

When I Have Fears that I May Cease to Be

When I have fears that I may cease to be
Before my pen has glean'd my teeming brain,
Before high pilèd books, in charact'ry,
Hold like rich garners the full-ripen'd grain;
When I behold, upon the night's starr'd face,
Huge cloudy symbols of a high romance,
And think that I may never live to trace
Their shadows, with the magic hand of chance;
And when I feel, fair creature of an hour,
That I shall never look upon thee more,
Never have relish in the faery power
Of unreflecting love—then on the shore
Of the wide world I stand alone, and think
Till Love and Fame to nothingness do sink.

—JOHN KEATS

The Tiger

Tiger, Tiger, burning bright
In the forests of the night,
What immortal hand or eye
Could frame thy fearful symmetry?

In what distant deeps or skies
Burnt the fire of thine eyes?
On what wings dare he aspire?
What the hand dare seize the fire?

And what shoulder, and what art,
Could twist the sinews of thy heart?
And when thy heart began to beat,
What dread hand? and what dread feet?

What the hammer? what the chain?
In what furnace was thy brain?
What the anvil? what dread grasp
Dare its deadly terrors clasp?

When the stars threw down their spears,
And watered heaven with their tears,
Did he smile his work to see?
Did he who made the Lamb make thee?

Tiger, Tiger, burning bright
In the forests of the night,
What immortal hand or eye
Dare frame thy fearful symmetry?

—WILLIAM BLAKE

Binsey Poplars Felled 1879

My aspens dear, whose airy cages quelled,
Quelled or quenched in leaves the leaping sun,
All felled, felled, are all felled;
  Of a fresh and following folded rank
         Not spared, not one
         That dandled a sandalled
  Shadow that swam or sank
On meadow and river and wind-wandering weed-winding
    bank.

O if we but knew what we do
  When we delve or hew—
  Hack and rack the growing green!
    Since country is so tender
  To touch, her being so slender,
  That, like this sleek and seeing ball
  But a prick will make no eye at all,
  Where we, even where we mean
        To mend her we end her,
  When we hew or delve:
After-comers cannot guess the beauty been.
  Ten or twelve, only ten or twelve
  Strokes of havoc unselve
      The sweet especial scene,
  Rural scene, a rural scene,
  Sweet especial rural scene.

—GERARD MANLEY HOPKINS

Dover Beach

The sea is calm tonight.
The tide is full, the moon lies fair
Upon the straits;—on the French coast the light
Gleams and is gone; the cliffs of England stand,
Glimmering and vast, out in the tranquil bay.
Come to the window, sweet is the night air!
Only, from the long line of spray
Where the sea meets the moon-blanched land,
Listen! you hear the grating roar
Of pebbles which the waves draw back, and fling,
At their return, up the high strand,
Begin, and cease, and then again begin,
With tremulous cadence slow, and bring
The eternal note of sadness in.

Sophocles long ago
Heard it on the Aegean, and it brought
Into his mind the turbid ebb and flow
Of human misery; we
Find also in the sound a thought,
Hearing it by this distant northern sea.
The Sea of Faith
Was once, too, at the full, and round earth's shore
Lay like the folds of a bright girdle furled.
But now I only hear
Its melancholy, long, withdrawing roar,
Retreating, to the breath
Of the night wind, down the vast edges drear
And naked shingles of the world.
Ah, love, let us be true
To one another! for the world, which seems
To lie before us like a land of dreams,
So various, so beautiful, so new,
Hath really neither joy, nor love, nor light,
Nor certitude, nor peace, nor help for pain;
And we are here as on a darkling plain
Swept with confused alarms of struggle and flight
Where ignorant armies clash by night.

—MATTHEW ARNOLD

Ode to the West Wind

I

O wild West Wind, thou breath of Autumn's being,
Thou, from whose unseen presence the leaves dead
Are driven, like ghosts from an enchanter fleeing,

Yellow, and black, and pale, and hectic red,
Pestilence-stricken multitudes: O thou,
Who chariotest to their dark wintry bed

The wingèd seeds, where they lie cold and low,
Each like a corpse within its grave, until
Thine azure sister of the spring shall blow

Her clarion o'er the dreaming earth, and fill
(Driving sweet buds like flocks to feed in air)
With living hues and odors plain and hill;

Wild Spirit, which art moving everywhere;
Destroyer and preserver; hear, Oh hear!

II

Thou on whose stream, 'mid the steep sky's commotion,
Loose clouds like earth's decaying leaves are shed,
Shook from the tangled boughs of Heaven and Ocean,

Angels of rain and lightning: there are spread
On the blue surface of thine airy surge,
Like the bright hair uplifted from the head

Of some fierce Maenad, even from the dim verge
Of the horizon to the zenith's height,
The locks of the approaching storm. Thou dirge

Of the dying year, to which this closing night
Will be the dome of a vast sepulcher,
Vaulted with all thy congregated might

Of vapors, from whose solid atmosphere
Black rain, and fire, and hail will burst: Oh hear!

Thou who didst waken from his summer dreams
The blue Mediterranean, where he lay,
Lulled by the coil of his crystalline streams.

Beside a pumice isle in Baiae's bay,
And saw in sleep old palaces and towers
Quivering within the wave's intenser day,

All overgrown with azure moss and flowers
So sweet, the sense faints picturing them! Thou
For whose path the Atlantic's level powers

Cleave themselves into chasms, while far below
The sea-blooms and the oozy woods which wear
The sapless foliage of the ocean, know

Thy voice, and suddenly grow gray with fear,
And tremble and despoil themselves: Oh hear!

IV

If I were a dead leaf thou mightest bear;
If I were a swift cloud to fly with thee;
A wave to pant beneath thy power, and share

The impulse of thy strength, only less free
Than thou, O uncontrollable! If even
I were as in my boyhood, and could be

The comrade of thy wanderings over heaven,
As then, when to outstrip thy skiey speed
Scarce seemed a vision; I would ne'er have striven

As thus with thee in prayer in my sore need.
Oh lift me as a wave, a leaf, a cloud!
I fall upon the thorns of life! I bleed!

A heavy weight of hours has chained and bowed
One too like thee: tameless, and swift, and proud.

V

Make me thy lyre, even as the forest is:
What if my leaves are falling like its own!
The tumult of thy mighty harmonies

Will take from both a deep, autumnal tone,
Sweet though in sadness. Be thou, spirit fierce,
My spirit! Be thou me, impetuous one!

Drive my dead thoughts over the universe
Like withered leaves to quicken a new birth!
And, by the incantation of this verse,

Scatter, as from an unextinguished hearth
Ashes and sparks, my words among mankind!
Be through my lips to unawakened earth

The trumpet of a prophecy! O, wind,
If Winter comes, can Spring be far behind?

                    —PERCY BYSSHE SHELLEY

Felix Randal

Felix Randal the farrier, O he is dead then? my duty all
    ended,
Who have watched his mould of man, big-boned and
    hardy-handsome
Pining, pining, till time when reason rambled in it and
    some
Fatal four disorders, fleshed there, all contended?
Sickness broke him. Impatient he cursed at first, but
    mended
Being anointed and all; though a heavenlier heart began
    some
Months earlier, since I had our sweet reprieve and ransom
Tendered to him. Ah well, God rest him all road ever he
    offended!
This seeing the sick endears them to us, us too it endears.
My tongue had taught thee comfort, touch had quenched
    thy tears,
Thy tears that touched my heart, child, Felix, poor Felix
    Randal;
How far from then forethought of, all thy more boisterous
    years,

When thou at the random grim forge, powerful amidst
    peers,
Didst fettle for the great grey drayhorse his bright and bat-
    tering sandal!

—GERARD MANLEY HOPKINS

The Force that Through
the Green Fuse Drives

The force that through the green fuse drives the flower
Drives my green age; that blasts the roots of tree
Is my destroyer.
And I am dumb to tell the crooked rose
My youth is bent by the same wintry fever.

The force that drives the water through the rocks
Drives my red blood; that dries the mouthing streams
Turns mine to wax.
And I am dumb to mouth unto my veins
How at the mountain spring the same mouth sucks.

The hand that whirls the water in the pool
Stirs the quicksand; that ropes the blowing wind
Hauls my shroud sail.
And I am dumb to tell the hanging man
How of my clay is made the hangman's lime.

The lips of time leech to the fountain head;
Love drips and gathers, but the fallen blood
Shall calm her sores.
And I am dumb to tell a weather's wind
How time has ticked a heaven round the stars.

And I am dumb to tell the lover's tomb
How at my sheet goes the same crooked worm.

—DYLAN THOMAS

Ode on a Grecian Urn

Thou still unravish'd bride of quietness,
   Thou foster-child of silence and slow time,
Sylvan historian, who canst thus express
   A flowery tale more sweetly than our rhyme:
What leaf-fring'd legend haunts about thy shape
   Of deities or mortals, or of both,
     In Tempe or the dales of Arcady?
What men or gods are these? What maidens loth?
   What mad pursuit? What struggle to escape?
     What pipes and timbrels? What wild ecstasy?

Heard melodies are sweet, but those unheard
   Are sweeter; therefore, ye soft pipes, play on;
Not to the sensual ear, but, more endear'd,
   Pipe to the spirit ditties of no tone:
Fair youth, beneath the trees, thou canst not leave
   Thy song, nor ever can those trees be bare;
     Bold Lover, never, never canst thou kiss
Though winning near the goal—yet, do not grieve;
   She cannot fade, though thou hast not thy bliss,
     For ever wilt thou love, and she be fair!

Ah, happy, happy boughs! that cannot shed
   Your leaves, nor ever bid the Spring adieu;
And, happy melodist, unwearied,
   For ever piping songs for ever new;
More happy love! more happy, happy love!
   For ever warm and still to be enjoy'd,
     For ever panting, and for ever young;
All breathing human passion far above,
   That leaves a heart high-sorrowful and cloy'd,
     A burning forehead, and a parching tongue.

Who are these coming to the sacrifice?
   To what green altar, O mysterious priest,
Lead'st thou that heifer lowing at the skies,
   And all her silken flanks with garlands dressed?
What little town by river or sea shore,
   Or mountain-built with peaceful citadel,
     Is emptied of this folk, this pious morn?

And, little town, thy streets for evermore
Will silent be; and not a soul to tell
Why thou art desolate, can e'er return.

O Attic shape! Fair attitude! with brede
Of marble men and maidens over wrought,
With forest branches and the trodden weed;
Thou, silent form, dost tease us out of thought
As doth eternity: Cold Pastoral!
When old age shall this generation waste,
Thou shalt remain, in midst of other woe
Than ours, a friend to man, to whom thou say'st,
"Beauty is truth, truth beauty,"—that is all
Ye know on earth, and all ye need to know.

—JOHN KEATS

Song: Stop All the Clocks

Stop all the clocks, cut off the telephone,
Prevent the dog from barking with a juicy
    bone,
Silence the pianos and with muffled drum
Bring out the coffin, let the mourners come.

Let aeroplanes circle moaning overhead
Scribbling on the sky the message He Is
    Dead,
Put crêpe bows round the white necks of the
    public doves,
Let the traffic policemen wear black cotton
    gloves.

He was my North, my South, my East and
    West,
My working week and my Sunday rest,
My noon, my midnight, my talk, my song;
I thought that love would last for ever: I was
    wrong.

The stars are not wanted now; put out every
   one:
Pack up the moon and dismantle the sun;
Pour away the ocean and sweep up the
   woods:
For nothing now can ever come to any good.
                                    —W. H. AUDEN

About the Poets

(Bracketed numbers refer to pages where poets' works appear in this book)

ADAMS, FRANKLIN P. (1881–1960). American newspaper columnist, humorist, and versifier. [18]

ARNOLD, MATTHEW (1822–1888). English essayist, inspector of schools, and poet. Arnold did not view the world with optimism, as Robert Browning did, but rather with courageous stoicism. [119]

AUDEN, W. H. (1907–   ). Perhaps the most skillful craftsman of all British poets writing today. His subjects are many and the variety of his verse forms is incredibly extensive. [111, 125]

BITTERMAN, HERBERT (1914–1944). Relatively unknown poet from Newark, New Jersey, whose untimely death at the age of twenty-nine cut short the promise of a brilliant career in acting, music, and writing. [1, 14, 86]

BLAKE, WILLIAM (1757–1827). Artist, poet, and engraver; lived in England during the early days of the Industrial Revolution, and spoke out against its abuses. Blake's poetry and engravings are based on a deep mysticism. [44, 117]

BOOTH, PHILIP (1925–   ). American poet from Maine who has recently been serving as poet-in-residence at Syracuse University. His two volumes of poetry are *Letter from a Distant Land* and *The Islanders*. [82]

BROWNING, ELIZABETH BARRETT (1806–1861). Wife of Robert Browning and a fine poet in her own right. Rudolph Besier's play, *The Barretts of Wimpole Street*, celebrates their courtship. [17]

BROWNING, ROBERT (1812–1889). English poet who wrote in the time of Queen Victoria. His poetry is dramatic and vigorous; his philosophy, optimistic. [6, 76]

BURNS, ROBERT (1759–1796). The plowboy of Scotland who became her most beloved poet. Hearty, good-humored, and romantic, Burns expressed the feelings of his people for all time. [55]

CARROLL, LEWIS (1829–1898). Pen name of Charles Lutwidge Dodgson, who was a lecturer in mathematics at Oxford University as well as the author of *Alice in Wonderland*. [101]

COLERIDGE, SAMUEL TAYLOR (1772–1834). English poet, critic, and philosopher whose poems manifest his deep interest in the supernatural. [51]

CRANE, STEPHEN (1871–1900). American novelist, short-story writer, and poet. His poems are often paradoxical and cynical. [58]

CUMMINGS, E. E. (1894–1962). American poet whose rejection of capitals and experiments with spacing and punctuation are designed not only to shock the reader, but also to guide him in his oral interpretation of the verse. [42]

DALY, THOMAS AUGUSTINE (1871–1948). Philadelphia newspaper columnist and writer of verse. His reputation rests largely on his dialect poems. [97]

DAVIES, W. H. (1871–1940). British poet who traveled as a hobo throughout England, Canada, and the United States. George Bernard Shaw discovered him and helped to make his poetry known. [48]

DE LA MARE, WALTER (1873–1956). English poet whose delicate lyrics and poems for children transform the ordinary into magic. [10, 74]

DICKINSON, EMILY (1830–1886). Probably America's most famous woman poet. She spent her life as a recluse in Amherst, Massachusetts, unknown as a poet except to her family and a few friends. [45, 56, 78, 94, 95, 96]

DRAYTON, MICHAEL (1563–1631). English lyric poet of Elizabethan times. [99]

FIELD, EUGENE (1850–1895). American journalist and versifier whose high-sprited poems have appealed to both children and adults. [35]

FIELDS, JAMES THOMAS (1817–1881). Publisher and editor of the *Atlantic Monthly*; an occasional dabbler in light verse. [58]

FITZGERALD, EDWARD (1809–1883). English poet who is chiefly remembered for his free translation of the *Rubáiyát*. This collection of quatrains was originally written by the Persian poet Omar Khayyám in the eleventh century. [65]

FROST, ROBERT (1875–1963). Most famous modern American poet; a grand old granite-type man, who became, through his poems, the voice of New England. [20, 74, 114]

GILBERT, WILLIAM S. (1836–1911). Famous librettist of comic opera, collaborator with the composer Arthur Sullivan in producing brilliant musical satires. [102]

HARDY, THOMAS (1840–1928). English novelist who was finally able to devote himself to poetry at the age of fifty-eight, when, as he said, he could afford to write it. [76]

HENLEY, WILLIAM ERNEST (1849–1903). English poet whose concern for courage and strength probably derived from his own bouts with serious illness. [5]

HODGSON, RALPH (1871–1962). A quiet man who let his lyrical poetry speak for him. Born in England, he spent his last years on a farm outside of Canton, Ohio. [89]

HOPKINS, GERARD MANLEY (1844–1889). English poet who was a Jesuit and a professor of Greek. His poems did not become known until fifty years after his death; now they are regarded as some of the best in the English language. [14, 108, 118, 122]

HOUSMAN, A. E. (1859–1936). English classical scholar and poet, whose *A Shropshire Lad* has been one of the most popular collections of verse in the twentieth century. [1, 15, 26, 46, 77, 102]

HUGHES, LANGSTON (1902–   ). American Negro poet, short-story writer, dramatist, and journalist. [75, 96]

HUNT, LEIGH (1784–1859). English poet and essayist, editor of a succession of magazines devoted to publishing the new writers of his day. [7]

JARRELL, RANDALL (1914–   ). American poet, teacher, and literary critic. After he served in the Army Air Corps during World War II, many of his poems evoked the horror and pathos of war. [108]

JOHNSON, JAMES WELDON (1871–1938). American Negro poet and author of *The Autobiography of an Ex-Coloured Man.* In addition to being a high-school principal and a member of the Florida bar, he served seven years as a United States Consul in Venezuela. [3]

JONSON, BEN (1573–1637). Poet and playwright of Elizabethan and Jacobean England, a writer of both satirical plays and tender love poems. [63]

KEATS, JOHN (1795–1821). Keats once stated in a letter that he expected to be remembered among the British poets after his death. Although he died of consumption at twenty-five, he is now considered one of the greatest of the Romantics. [109, 117, 124]

KILMER, JOYCE (1886–1918). Poet from New Jersey whose name survives mainly because of the poem "Trees." [47]

KIPLING, RUDYARD (1865–1936). Born in Bombay, India, his verse and tales are stirring and nostalgic affirmations of the days of glory of the nineteenth-century British Empire. [26, 34, 84, 90]

LEIGH, HENRY SAMBROOKE (1837–1883). British writer of humorous verse. [73]

LINDSAY, VACHEL (1879–1931). Illinois writer who preached "a gospel beauty" through his poetry. His verse often portrays American folk heroes, historical personages, and popular figures of his day. [23]

LOWELL, AMY (1874–1925). American poet, essayist, biographer, critic. Miss Lowell was one of the leaders of the Imagists, a group of poets who revolted against traditional verse forms and advocated the use of precise images. [48]

McCRAE, JOHN (1872–1918). Canadian poet and medical officer, who, as so many of his generation, hoped that World War I would be the war to end all wars; killed in action. [66]

MacNEICE, LOUIS (1907–   ). Contemporary British poet, born in Belfast. Like that of Auden and Spender, his poetry records the contemporary scene; his language is strong and direct. [107]

MAGEE, JOHN GILLESPIE (1922–1941). Young American killed in World War II, whose fame rests largely on "High Flight." He was a pilot-officer with the Royal Canadian Air Force. [25]

MARKHAM, EDWIN (1852–1940). American poet whose most important poem, "The Man with the Hoe," was inspired by a painting on the same subject by the French artist Jean François Millet. [100]

MASEFIELD, JOHN (1878–   ). Poet Laureate of England

since 1930; his early wanderings resulted in many poems about sailors and the sea. [85]

MILLAY, EDNA ST. VINCENT (1892–1950). First-rate American poet from her college days, when she wrote "Renascence"; frequently identified with the artists and writers of Greenwich Village in the first quarter of this century. [29, 36, 56, 62]

MORLEY, CHRISTOPHER (1890–1957). American essayist, novelist, verse writer, who, viewing people with wit and irony, never discarded warmth and tenderness. [97]

NASH, OGDEN (1902–   ). Popular American versifier whose tricky rhymes and sense of humor have entertained thousands of readers. [42]

NOYES, ALFRED (1880–1958). English poet whose spirited poems often depict events or periods in English history. [67]

OWEN, WILFRED (1893–1918). English poet, killed in action during World War I. His poetry was published in 1920 after his death. [24]

PARKER, DOROTHY (1893–   ). American writer of sophisticated verse and entertaining short stories. [2]

POE, EDGAR ALLAN (1809–1849). American poet and writer of tales, whose work has achieved great popularity in both America and Europe. He is noted for his strong rhythms. [11, 16, 37, 43]

RANSOM, JOHN CROWE (1888–   ). Southerner whose elegant poems are concerned with the pathos of everyday life. He is also an editor, critic, and college professor. [113]

RILEY, JAMES WHITCOMB (1849–1916). American poet whose rustic verse, often in dialect, achieved a widespread popularity. [88]

ROBINSON, EDWIN ARLINGTON (1869–1935). American poet who described an imaginary village in Maine called "Tilbury Town," and peopled it with some of modern poetry's most unforgettable characters. [78]

ROETHKE, THEODORE (1908–   ). Modern American poet, professor of English at the University of Washington. He has received two Guggenheim Fellowships, an award by the American Academy of Arts and Letters, and the Pulitzer Prize for his excellent poetry. [36]

SANDBURG, CARL (1878–   ). American poet, singer and collector of American folksongs, best-known biographer of Abraham Lincoln. [2, 26, 63, 95]

SARETT, LEW (1888–1954). American poet who combined teaching English in the winter with living among the Chippewa Indians in Minnesota in the summer; many of his poems are about this tribe. [19]

SEEGER, ALAN (1888–1916). American poet who foresaw his own death as a soldier in World War I. [46]

SERVICE, ROBERT W. (1874–1958). Canadian poet who celebrated the days of the Gold Rush in the Yukon with roistering ballads. [79]

SHAKESPEARE, WILLIAM (1564–1616). The most famous English poet and playwright of all time. [20, 61, 116]

SHELLEY, PERCY BYSSHE (1792–1822). English Romantic poet noted for his poems of social protest as well as for his beautiful love lyrics and odes to nature. [6, 114, 120]

SILL, EDWARD ROWLAND (1841–1887). Minor American poet whose poems have served as moral inspirations. [83]

STEPHENS, JAMES (1882–1950). Modern Irish poet whose simple, direct poetry ranges from the serious to the playful. He is also well known for his novel, *The Crock of Gold.* [6]

STEVENSON, ROBERT LOUIS (1850–1894). Scottish writer of adventure stories and verse. *A Child's Garden of Verses* contains poetry of charming simplicity. [71]

TEASDALE, SARA (1884–1933). Born in Missouri, traveled throughout Europe and the Mideast, and finally settled down in New York City. Her poems are tender, romantic, and highly polished. [98, 99]

TENNYSON, ALFRED LORD (1809–1892). Poet Laureate of England in the reign of Queen Victoria. [71]

THAYER, ERNEST LAWRENCE (1863–1940). American journalist and versifier whose poem "Casey at the Bat" is better know than he is. [8]

THOMAS, DYLAN (1914–1953). A wild, exuberant Welshman who stirred poetry lovers of the 1940's and 1950's not only with his poetry but also with his marvelous readings of it. His recordings are still very popular. [123]

WARD, HERMAN M. (1914–   ). Professor of English, Trenton State College, and an editor of high-school literature anthologies. His own poetry has been published in *Descant, College English,* and other magazines. [57]

WHITMAN, WALT (1819–1892). Modern free verse received its impetus from the free-wheeling, intoxicating rhythms of Whitman's songs of America in the nineteenth century. [22, 87]

WHITTIER, JOHN GREENLEAF (1807–1892). Largely self-educated American poet who celebrated his rural childhood in his verse. [53]

WOLFE, HUMBERT (1885–1940). Twentieth-century English poet who wrote with a dexterous combination of charm and irony. [75]

WORDSWORTH, WILLIAM (1770–1850). English Romantic poet who believed that man would find the best reasons for living when he was close to nature. [18, 44, 47]

WYLIE, ELINOR (1885–1928). Modern American poet, a great craftsman whose poems are written with skill and polish. [62]

YEATS, WILLIAM BUTLER (1865–1939). Ireland's greatest modern poet, considered by some to be the greatest of all twentieth-century poets. His subjects are extremely varied, from moving simple tales about the Irish peasantry to abstruse and highly complicated treatments of the plight of the sensitive individual in the modern world. [115]

Index of Titles

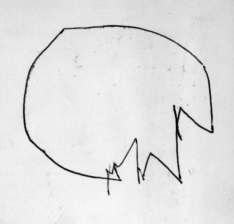